Translated Texts for Historians
Latin Series IV

Gregory of Tours
Glory of the Confessors

Translated with an introduction by
RAYMOND VAN DAM

Liverpool
University
Press

First published 1988 by
Liverpool University Press
PO Box 147, Liverpool, L69 3BX

British Library Cataloguing-in-Publication Data
Gregory, *Saint, Bishop of Tours*
  [De gloria confessorum. *English*]
  Glory of the confessors.
  1. Saints — Biographies — Early works
  [De gloria confessorum. *English*]
  I. Title II. Series
  270

ISBN 0 85323 226 1

Printed in Great Britain by
Oxford University Press Printing House

CONTENTS

PREFACE

Gregory of Tours was modest enough to concede that others would build upon his writings; translators likewise ought to hope that their readers will be stimulated to learn more about the original writings and their historical context. The series "Translated Texts for Historians" is therefore to be commended for encouraging the initial translations into English of important works from Late Antiquity. A Fellowship from the National Endowment for the Humanities made it possible for me to consider translating both Gregory's *Glory of the confessors* (in this volume) and his *Glory of the martyrs* (in a companion volume). Gillian Clark, Christa Mee, and Ian Wood have commented on the introduction, translation, and notes. The University of Michigan now offers access to a computer and laser printer. The National Humanities Center provided the appropriate atmosphere; in the shade of its forest all who have been honored to be Fellows have found, like Johannis the recluse, an opportunity to read and write.

University of Michigan
June 1988

ABBREVIATIONS

ACW	Ancient Christian Writers (Westminster).
CChrL	*Corpus Christianorum*, series latina (Turnhout).
CSEL	*Corpus scriptorum ecclesisticorum latinorum* (Vienna).
LCL	Loeb Classical Library (Cambridge, Massachusetts, and London).
MGH	*Monumenta Germaniae historica* (Berlin, Hannover, and Leipzig).
AA	Auctores antiquissimi.
SRM	Scriptores rerum merovingicarum.
NPNF	A select library of Nicene and Post-Nicene Fathers of the Christian Church, 2nd series (reprinted Grand Rapids).
PL	*Patrologia latina* (Paris); and Supplementa, ed. A. Hamman (Paris, 1958-1974).
PLRE	*The prosopography of the later Roman empire.* Vol.2, ed. J.R.Martindale (Cambridge, 1980).
SChr	*Sources chrétiennes* (Paris).

Writings of Gregory of Tours:

GC	*Glory of the confessors*
GM	*Glory of the martyrs*
HF	*Histories* ["History of the Franks"]
VJ	*Suffering and miracles of the martyr St Julian*
VM	*Miracles of the bishop St Martin*
VP	*Life of the fathers*

INTRODUCTION

In 573 Gregory became bishop of Tours. This promotion was not unexpected, because since the early sixth century several of his ancestors had served as bishops throughout central and southern Gaul. Gregory himself was born in the late 530s and grew up in Clermont, where Gallus, his father's brother, was bishop. During his episcopacy Gallus enhanced the cult of St Julian by instituting an annual pilgrimage to the saint's shrine at Brioude, another town in the Auvergne. Gregory's entire family was specially attached to the cult of St Julian, and Gregory eventually considered himself a "foster son" of the saint whom he thought of as his "special patron". Gregory's family also had distinctive connections with Tours and its cult of St Martin. In 563 Gregory completed a difficult pilgrimage to the tomb of St Martin in his church outside Tours where the saint cured him of a severe fever. By then Tours had become virtually a family see. The current bishop was a cousin of Gregory's mother, and after Gregory succeeded him, he could boast that all but five of his predecessors had been members of his family. During the last twenty years of his life until his death (probably) in 594, Gregory was therefore maintaining both the family's prominence in the ecclesiastical hierarchy and its consequential links with Tours and the cult of St Martin.[1]

Service in the ecclesiastical hierarchy, however, only added to the family's local influence. One of Gregory's grandfathers had still claimed the rank of senator, a prestigious title that revived memories of five centuries of Roman rule in Gaul. But by the later fifth century the Roman empire had already vanished from most of Gaul as various barbarian leaders had gradually established small kingdoms. The most successful had been Clovis, who had first ruthlessly made himself king

---

[1] For details about Gregory and his family, see Pietri (1983) 247-64, and Van Dam (1985) 202-17; important introductory surveys to Gregory and his writings include Krusch (1951), Buchner (1955), and Vollmann (1983).

of all the Franks in northern Gaul. His most significant military success had been his victory in 507 over the Visigoths, who consequently abandoned most of their possessions in southern and central Gaul and moved into Spain. At some point during his reign Clovis also astutely converted to orthodox catholic Christianity. Much of Roman Gaul had already been converted to catholic Christianity during the previous century. By the time of his death in 511, Clovis had therefore consolidated the rule of the Franks over much of Gaul and had earned the loyalty of many catholic bishops and their Roman congregations.[2]

As Gregory grew to adulthood in the middle of the sixth century this kingdom of the Franks sometimes looked to be on the verge of disintegration. All legitimate sons of the ruling Merovingian family expected to receive portions of the kingdom to rule as their own mini-kingdoms. These mini-kingdoms generally had territorial cores, but they also often included control over individual cities scattered around Gaul. Usually several kings were ruling concurrently; Gregory had to deal with sons, grandsons, and great-grandsons of Clovis. Usually too these various kings were feuding with each other and sometimes making war on each other.

Wars were in fact perhaps the primary emphasis of Gregory's writings, and they included not only the wars of kings with their enemies, but also the wars of martyrs with pagans and of the catholic churches with heretics [HF I praef.]. During his tenure as bishop of Tours Gregory wrote several works about the wars of kings, saints, and churchmen. Near the end of his career he listed his important works [HF X.31]: "I have written ten books of histories, seven books of miracles, and one book about the life of the fathers. I wrote one volume of commentary on the book of Psalms and one book about the liturgical offices of the church."[3] He also translated an account of the

---

[2] Three excellent and concise introductory discussions of early medieval Gaul are Wallace-Hadrill (1967), James (1982), and Geary (1988). The best surveys of the history of the church in Gaul are Griffe (1964-1966), who covers the Roman period through the fifth century, and Wallace-Hadrill (1983), who covers the Frankish period; see also the relevant sections in Baus, Beck, Ewig and Vogt (1980).

[3] Gregory's title for his book on the liturgical offices was somewhat misleading, since the treatise contained first a section describing seven man-made wonders of the world and seven natural wonders, and then a section describing the

Seven Sleepers in Ephesus,[4] wrote a preface for a collection of liturgical masses [*HF* II.22], and condensed a book about the miracles of St Andrew.[5] With the exception of his commentary on the Psalms, of which only the introduction, a table of contents, and a few fragments are extant,[6] and his preface for the book of masses, his important literary works have survived. His ten books of histories, now commonly (although misleadingly) known as the "History of the Franks" [*HF*], are certainly the most familiar to modern readers, in part because they provide the most detailed continuous narrative of events in sixth-century Gaul, in part too because they have been well translated into English (and other modern languages).[7]

In contrast, Gregory's seven books of miracles and one book on the life of the fathers are much less familiar to modern readers. When Gregory listed these books again in the preface to one of them, he counted them as eight books of miracles [*GC* praef.], which is how modern scholars now also customarily consider them. In Gregory's own sequence these eight books included:

---

movement of the stars that was intended to enable men to celebrate liturgical offices at the appropriate hours during the night: ed. B.Krusch, *MGH*, SRM 1.2 (1885) 857-72; first section trans. McDermott (1975) 209-18.

[4] See his *Passio sanctorum martyrum septem dormientium apud Ephysum*, ed. B.Krusch, *MGH*, SRM 1.2 (1885) 848-53, and again in SRM 7 (1920) 761-9; and trans. McDermott (1975) 199-206. Gregory also wrote a short account of the Seven Sleepers [*GM* 94].

[5] For a large collection of miracle stories about St Andrew, see the *Liber de miraculis beati Andreae apostoli* [*MA*], ed. M.Bonnet, *MGH*, SRM 1.2 (1885) 826-46. In the preface to this collection the author stated that he had found a book about the miracles of St Andrew that he intended to condense into one small volume because some people had dismissed it as apocryphal on the basis of its verbosity. Bonnet, o.c. 821-2, argues that Gregory was the author of this condensed volume; despite lingering scepticism, others have agreed that the *MA* is Gregory's adaptation of a fourth-century Latin version: see Zelzer (1977), and Prieur (1981).

[6] Ed. B.Krusch, *MGH*, SRM 1.2 (1885) 874-7.

[7] The best editions are by W.Arndt, *MGH*, SRM 1.1 (1885), and by B.Krusch and W.Levison, *MGH*, SRM 1.1 (1937-1951); Goffart (1987), is an important discussion of title and textual history. The most accessible English translations are Dalton (1927) and Thorpe (1974).

1. one book entitled *Glory of the martyrs* [*GM*], consisting of stories about martyrs and the miracles they or their relics performed;[8]

2. one book entitled *Suffering and miracles of the martyr St Julian* [*VJ*], consisting of stories about the saint and his shrine at Brioude;

3-6. four books entitled *Miracles of the bishop St Martin* [*VM* 1-4], consisting of stories about the patron saint of Tours and the miracles he performed, primarily at Tours, before and during Gregory's episcopacy;[9]

7. one book entitled *Life of the fathers* [*VP*], consisting of a series of short biographies of illustrious men and women in the church, almost all of whom lived during the sixth century and among whom were some of Gregory's own relatives;[10] and

8. one book entitled *Glory of the confessors* [*GC*], consisting of stories about confessors and the miracles they or their relics performed.

Only some of these books have been translated into English; this volume is the first complete translation into English of the *Glory of the confessors*.

Gregory wrote most, if not all, of his surviving works during the years of his episcopacy. His book about the glory of the confessors was perhaps one of his last. In it he mentioned that he had already written his third book about the miracles of St Martin [*GC* 6]; that third book ended with a miracle that happened in November 587, and the fourth book began with a miracle that happened in July 588.[11] In *GC* 104 Gregory mentioned the death and funeral of Radegund, who had died in August 587. In *GC* 93 he emphasized that Charimeris, who became bishop of Verdun in 588, was still "now" a royal secretary.

---

[8] Translated by Van Dam (1988), with introduction and notes.

[9] McDermott (1975) 129-95, has translated *VM* 1, *VP* 6-7, and the prefaces to all the books of miracles. Since Gregory once begged that his books be kept intact [*HF* X.31], he would perhaps not have approved of only selections in translation.

[10] Translated by James (1985), with introduction and notes.

[11] For the chronology of the miracle stories in *VM* 2-4, see Schlick (1966), and Heinzelmann (1981).

These internal allusions and cross references therefore suggest that Gregory was writing his book about the confessors during the winter and spring of 587-588.

But as with most of his books, Gregory also constantly supplemented and revised what he had already written. In *GC* 94 he mentioned a *Vita* of Albinus that his friend Fortunatus had "recently" written. Fortunatus had dedicated this *Vita* to bishop Domitianus of Angers, who died before 572. Unless Gregory could disregard the passage of over sixteen years, he may have written this chapter years earlier perhaps when he first became bishop in 573 and then simply reused it later without properly updating it. In another chapter he mentioned a "recent" civil war in Spain that had been fought out during the early 580s [*GC* 12]. In *GC* 60 he recorded some miracles that he had learned about from a "trustworthy man" who may well have been his deacon Agiulf, who had stopped in Lyon after visiting Rome in 590. He mentioned his archdeacon Probatus [*GC* 24], who could have become archdeacon at Tours only after his predecessor became bishop of Poitiers in 591. Gregory also intended to include three chapters [*GC* 105-107] that no manuscripts preserve; perhaps his own death in 594 prevented him from writing those chapters. It is therefore likely that not only had Gregory collected these stories throughout his life, he was probably also writing them down over the years too, with perhaps one concentrated burst of writing and revising around early 588: "I recall a story I heard years ago" [*GC* 96]. He eventually inserted cross references to some of the *Vitae* included in his *VP* [*GC* 15, 24, 25, 38, 92], and he obviously wrote, or at least rewrote, the preface toward the end of his career, since in its final paragraph he listed all his books of miracles [cf. *GC* 44].[12]

It is perhaps to be expected that there is therefore no chronological pattern to this collection of stories about confessors, their cults, and their miracles. Gregory began with a story about a miracle performed by angels as an evident parallel to stories about the miracles of Jesus Christ that had initiated his book about the martyrs. He then included a

---

[12] For detailed arguments about the dates of composition of the various books of miracles, see Monod (1872) 41-5, who dates the *GC* to c.587-588 and its preface to 594, and especially Krusch (1885) 451-6, who stresses Gregory's frequent revisions.

story about the power of St Hilary, the bishop of Poitiers in the mid-fourth century who is in fact one of the earliest figures in the history of the Gallic church about whom we have adequate reliable information, and another story about bishop Eusebius of Vercelli, a contemporary of Hilary who was also one of the few non-Gallic saints Gregory mentioned in this book. Thereafter Gregory grouped his stories geographically, with stories about particular cities clustered together. The largest cluster of stories focused, predictably, on his episcopal see of Tours [*GC* 4-25], followed in order by stories about Limoges, his home town of Clermont [*GC* 29-36], Dijon, Bordeaux, Cieutat, Poitiers, Saintes, Lyon, Troyes, Autun, Bourges, Chalon-sur-Saône, Paris, Trier, and Limoges again. Within these clusters Gregory allowed himself to digress elsewhere, if the stories still concerned the same saint, and between the clusters he included stories from other Gallic cities. Such an arrangement obviously made it easy for Gregory to insert stories about particular shrines or cities as he collected them; it also makes it difficult for modern scholars to distinguish any chronological layers in the composition of the book.

For information about people and events in the past Gregory often used books and written records. Sometimes he referred to *Vitae* as if he had read them [*GC* 2, 22, 26, 45, 57, 70, 76, 87, 93, 94, 108]; other times he referred to *Vitae* he had not read [*GC* 35, 44]. In a few cases he relied upon previous research and referred to his own books [*GC* 24, 25, 38]. Once he referred to books that he had in fact attributed to the wrong author [*GC* 108]

But since Gregory also felt, as he explicitly stated in the case of St Martin [*GC* 6], that earlier writers had simply omitted events about the lives of saints, he had no hesitation about supplementing his knowledge of past events and people with oral traditions. As he insisted in his preface, he could not remain silent about events from the past that trustworthy men had told him. Occasionally Gregory specified his informants. They included old men at Clermont [*GC* 5], bishop Eufronius of Tours [*GC* 18-19], and an abbot from Autun [*GC* 96]. But usually his informants remained anonymous, and Gregory simply introduced his stories about past miracles with a reference to current opinion, a general report, or a timeworn account: "it is common knowledge among everyone" [*GC* 66].

For information about events that happened during or shortly before his lifetime, Gregory seems to have used hardly any written records [cf. *GC* 22]. Instead he relied almost exclusively upon oral traditions that included both stories he heard from informants and plain gossip. His informants for contemporary miracles included his mother [*GC* 3, 84], his friend Aredius [*GC* 9-10], his archdeacon Probatus [*GC* 24], abbot Brachio [*GC* 38], various bishops and clerics [*GC* 29, 40, 77, 85], and people whom saints had healed [*GC* 28, 82, 101]. Gregory was clearly willing to talk with anyone; in one instance [*GC* 8] he wished that the horse who had witnessed a miracle could tell him about it! Often he seems to have initiated discussion of miracles by asking questions [cf. *GC* 9], and often his questions focused on specific relics or tombs that he visited and about which he wished to learn more. Many of the stories Gregory included were therefore second- or third-hand; others had collected or invented them as etiological legends that explained the origin or efficacy of their shrines and relics, and Gregory now simply recorded the stories once he heard them.[13]

This assortment of stories can easily leave the impression that Gregory was blissfully naive and gullible, distinguished more by his curiosity than by his critical judgement. In the case of one bishop, for example, he stressed that since there were no written records at all, he had to rely upon the reports of local clerics in order to say something [*GC* 44]. In another instance Gregory claimed verification for a story merely by noting that many people repeated it [*GC* 109]. But Gregory's curiosity and dedication also sometimes turned him into an amateur archaeologist and epigrapher. He made deductions about some saints on the basis of the scenes carved on their tombs or the appearance of the tombs [*GC* 34, 41], and he examined the inscriptions on tombs and doors [*GC* 35, 61, 103]. Once he even acknowledged ignorance and conceded that neither gossip nor a written document could identify the girl in a tomb [*GC* 34]. For in the end it was more important that men have their achievements recorded in heaven [*GC* 35]; God could adequately compensate for Gregory's deficiencies as an historian.

Because Gregory relied largely upon oral traditions for both past and contemporary events, his book about the confessors provides little

---

[13] For discussion of Gregory's sources and his reliability as an historian, see Kurth (1919) II:117-206.

reliable information about the early history of Christianity in Gaul. He recorded some traditions about third-century bishops and saints, although their accuracy is dubious [*GC* 4, 27, 29, 79]. He had more information about the fourth century, largely because of the prominence and importance of bishop Hilary of Poitiers and bishop Martin of Tours. In particular Gregory included a series of apparently apocryphal stories about bishop Martin [*GC* 4-10, 22, 45, 56]. For the fifth century Gregory again had comparatively more traditions to record, perhaps because "the time of the Huns" [*GC* 71], as well as the invasions of other barbarian tribes into Gaul, had deeply impressed contemporaries and provided a conspicuous reference point for subsequent oral traditions. But most of the people Gregory mentioned lived during the sixth century, and most of the miracles happened then; so in terms of both events and traditions the *GC* was a remarkably contemporary book.

It was also a notably parochial book that probably well reflected the limited geographical horizons of Gregory himself. In contrast to his book about the martyrs, many of whom had lived in the East, this book about the confessors mentioned only one eastern saint. In fact, the chapter about Symeon, a stylite saint who lived on his pillar near Antioch during the fifth century [*GC* 26], seems quite out of place sandwiched between chapters about a sixth-century abbot at Tours and a third-century bishop of Limoges. Usually when Gregory recorded events outside Gaul, there was a Gallic connection. He mentioned one bishop from Italy, probably because some of his relics were now to be found in Gregory's mother's house [*GC* 3], and he included some stories from Spain that followed from his discussion of the cult of St Martin [*GC* 12-14] and from Rome that involved a Gallic cleric [*GC* 62]. He also discussed Paulinus of Nola, a Gallic aristocrat who had once met St Martin before becoming a bishop in Italy [*GC* 108]. Excepting one other chapter recording a miracle that happened "somewhere in a port on the sea" [*GC* 109], the other stories all focused on Gallic cities.

Of these Gallic cities, Clermont and its vicinity were important as the region of Gregory's youth, and many of the stories he recorded about its shrines were based on traditions he had heard or experiences he had had while he was growing up [*GC* 30, "during my youth"]. But once Gregory was cured at the tomb of St Martin in 563 [*VM* 1.32-3], and even more so after he became bishop there in 573, Tours was for him the most important city in Gaul. In his perspective, other Gallic cities and other saints' cults seem to have surrounded his see in a series of concentric arcs. Gregory was most familiar with cities in central Gaul, to many of which he travelled during his life;[14] but in the *GC* he also recorded stories he had heard from cities as far north as Maastricht and Trier, as far west as Nantes and Rennes, as far south as Bordeaux, Cieutat, and Embrun, and as far east as Lyon and Chalon-sur-Saône. Significantly, as the episcopal guardian of the see of St Martin Gregory's interest in, knowledge of, and travels to other Gallic cities seems to have approximated closely to the influence of the cult of St Martin. A map plotting the cities with which Gregory was familiar, either firsthand through visiting or secondhand by report, might well correspond to maps plotting both the origins of pilgrims who travelled to the tomb of St Martin at Tours and the diffusion of shrines elsewhere dedicated to the saint.[15]

From the contemporary and parochial aspects of this book about the confessors it also follows that the *GC* was an intimately personal book. In fact, because Gregory had visited many of the shrines where he heard stories, had seen the relics, or had been a direct participant in or eyewitness to some of the events, this collection of the miracles of the confessors was one of his most autobiographical books. When Gregory visited various shrines, he often did so because of some personal or familial connections. At Lyon he was escorted around the various shrines by bishop Nicetius, his great-uncle, who told him a story about another bishop [*GC* 61]. Since Gregory also recorded miracles that St Nicetius worked after his death [*GC* 60], his great-uncle is an interesting case of someone who was both an informant for and a subject of the *GC*. At Dijon where Gregory received a cure for blisters on his hands, he was also visiting a see where a great-grandfather and another great-uncle had been bishops and where his own brother had been a priest [*GC* 43]. His mother seems to have accompanied him to Chalon-sur-Saône [*GC* 84]. When Gregory visited Auxerre, he went in

---

[14] For lists of the cities Gregory visited, see Monod (1872) 36-7, Kurth (1919) II:149-50, and Vieillard-Troiekouroff (1976) 455, with map at p.454.

[15] For the origins of pilgrims, see the map in Lelong (1960) 233, with the complete discussion in Pietri (1983) 521-99. For the shrines of St Martin, see the map in Vieillard-Troiekouroff (1976) 448, with the discussion of Ewig (1961).

the company of bishop Avitus of Clermont, who had once been one of his teachers [*GC* 40, *VP* 2 praef.].

Some of the stories also derived from Gregory's personal experiences and thus indicate his lifelong commitment to cults of saints. Gregory rarely mentioned his father, who seems to have been a generation older than Gregory's mother and who died when Gregory was still a boy. But once the young Gregory had been able to relieve his father's gout by applying a remedy he had learned about in a vision [*GC* 39]. Perhaps when he was young Gregory had listened to "old men" at Clermont telling stories about various saints [*GC* 5, 30] and watched as people were healed at shrines or treated saints with disrespect [*GC* 32, 35]. Once he became bishop of Tours, however, he became the guardian not only of the cult of St Martin, but also of traditions about the saint. Gregory felt compelled to register those traditions, because the saint's contemporary miracles proved the historicity of his past miracles [*GC* 6]. He therefore recorded anecdotes about St Martin that are elsewhere unattested, among them stories about a stone on which the saint had sat [*GC* 6], a tree he had put upright and a vine he had planted [*GC* 7, 10], oratories in which he had prayed [*GC* 4, 8], places he had visited [*GC* 5, 45], and various students of the saint [*GC* 22, 45, 56]. He then supplemented those traditions by recording contemporary miracles: "I recall that this happened during my lifetime" [*GC* 6]. He also contributed to the cult of St Martin by dedicating a new oratory at Tours with his relics as well as those of other saints [*GC* 20]. For Gregory always took care to extend his contacts with saints by visiting various shrines elsewhere, and even received miraculous cures at them [*GC* 45, 65, 73]. One of his most prized relics was the staff of St Medard from Soissons [*GC* 93].

In this book about the miracles of confessors Gregory rather strangely never defined who confessors were and how these particular saints had come to be ranked as confessors. This reticence might perhaps be another indication that this book was a late composition, since elsewhere he had defined confessors and so perhaps took it for granted that others would know. Martyrs were people, usually from past centuries, who had witnessed for their faith during persecutions often by suffering and dying; confessors, among them Gregory's contemporaries, had had to create their own opportunities for persecution. "Because a moment of persecution did not stimulate them to martyrdom, the confessors of Christ served as persecutors of themselves and applied the various tortures of abstinence so as to be considered worthy of God; they mortified their bodies so as to live for Christ alone" [*VP* 2 praef.]. This definition of confessors essentially stressed disciplined attitudes and rigorous behavior, and as such it was similar to Gregory's redefinition of martyrdom, whose relevance he had recast not in terms of physical suffering but in terms of moral resistance: "by resisting vices you will be considered a martyr" [*GM* 106].[16] By "persecuting" themselves confessors became contemporary "martyrs". Because Gregory's definition of confessors was not dependent upon particular circumstances, its potential application was considerable; and in fact, his collection included stories not only about great bishops and abbots, but also about the "Two Lovers" [*GC* 31], an anonymous monk [*GC* 37], a woman who retrieved a martyr's sandal [*GC* 63], a hermit who died after he fell from an apple tree [*GC* 80], and another old hermit who cooked his food in a wooden pot [*GC* 96].

In some of Gregory's other books he had presented saints as exemplars of correct behavior and as the embodiments of proper virtues. In the *GC* Gregory also narrated some stories "for the instruction of believers" [*GC* 20], and he sometimes explicitly encouraged certain attitudes such as chastity, generosity, and respect for the clergy [*GC* 30] and condemned others: "I ask that you who read these words cease from these activities, cease and do not participate in such behavior!" [*GC* 110]. One story even reads as if it may have been used as a homily during the celebration of the liturgy. This story began and ended with a passage (*lectio*) from the Bible that Gregory then elaborated in terms of the life and career of the saint [*GC* 108]. Through their own exemplary lives these confessor saints therefore proved that it was possible to imitate, equal, and even surpass the lives of earlier martyrs and saints. Yet overall this book about the confessors was less didactic than Gregory's collection of *Vitae* of saints, the *VP*; in those *Vitae* he intended to expand some of the brief accounts in his *GC* [*VP* praef.], and in the prefaces to each of the *Vitae* he had discussed and promoted various virtues. It was also less liturgical than his book about martyrs, the *GM*, parts of which may have been used during the celebration of

---

[16] Delehaye (1927) 74-121, discusses the relationship between martyr and confessor.

martyr saints' festivals. In fact, at the conclusion of this collection of stories about the confessors Gregory seems to have imagined that people would read the book privately, rather than hear it being read aloud in public [*GC* 110].

Gregory instead emphasized what these confessor saints could do for people who respected and honored them after their deaths [*GC* 44]. Because of their distinguished lives, these saints had become "friends of God" [*GC* 21, 44, 100] who now "lived with Christ" in Paradise [*GC* 52, 85]: "with the other saints he flourishes in heaven like a palm tree" [*GC* 50]. These saints therefore served as mediators with God [*GC* 2] whose intercession could channel his divine power to assist people [*GC* 28]. More specifically, for cities saints served as "special patrons" [*GC* 65, 68] who warded off both enemy attacks and the spread of the plague. For individuals saints protected possessions entrusted to their guardianship [*GC* 3] and supported people against accusations: one saint literally reached out from his tomb to embrace a man being threatened by a judge [*GC* 61; cf. 66]. The most evident way for saints to exhibit their power was through the miracles that happened usually at their tombs: "the saint continually demonstrates through his miracles that he lives in eternity" [*GC* 15].

To activate this miraculous power all people had to do was pay their respects and ask for the saints' assistance: "have pity on us, confessor of God" [*GC* 45]. Gregory's collection of stories was intended both to illustrate that proper respect and to promote it by concrete examples. In this book about the confessors he occasionally referred to the notion of *rusticitas*, a word that he used in various senses. One sense was fairly literal, since *rustici* were simply peasants or woodsmen who lived a rustic life in the countryside [*GC* 30, 62]. Another sense carried intellectual and cultural overtones, so that *rusticitas* could imply ignorance of high, classical culture and in particular of grammatically correct Latin. In this sense most people in Gaul were "rustics", since familiarity with classical literature and correct Latin had become increasingly restricted in Frankish Gaul.[17] Gregory was generally sympathetic to this sort of ignorance, not least because he could even accuse himself of "rusticity" by conceding that people might rightly

---

[17] Le Goff (1980), and Stock (1983) 27-8.

criticize his own literary gracelessness [*GC* praef.]. Yet, although he was no doubt unable to improve his style and syntax even if he had wished, Gregory perhaps preferred to write in this "rustic" style. As his mother once reminded him, at least people understood him [*VM* 1 praef.]: "few understand a rhetorician talking about philosophy, but many understand a man speaking simply" [*HF* praef.]. Gregory's "rustic" style therefore matched the "rusticity" of many members of his congregation.

But another, more highly charged sense of the word conjured up pejorative religious and moral overtones; what Gregory in this sense often referred to as *cruda rusticitas* implied both the rejection of Christianity and improper, if not clearly immoral, behavior and attitudes. Even as he provided models of exemplary behavior in the lives of the confessor saints, Gregory also provided models of improper behavior in his examples of people who perjured themselves at the tombs of saints or simply failed to respect the saints. Because of their "coarse rusticity" some people rejected a bishop's preaching of Christianity or refused to initiate a cult at a saint's tomb [*GC* 2, 29], one man perjured himself at a saint's tomb [*GC* 28], and another man decided to brew beer during a saint's festival [*GC* 80]. This sense of the word tended to be rather dismissive and callous; as far as Gregory was concerned, these disrespectful people actually deserved to suffer misfortune: "O coarse rusticity, because you always murmur against God and his friends, you receive catastrophe upon yourself" [*GC* 80]. Since bishops and other clerics tended to cast themselves as the guardians of saints' cults, they could also impose this distinction between proper and improper behavior to their own advantage. So one further purpose behind the *GC* might well have been an attempt to define and enforce correct behavior and proper attitudes by emphasizing their opposites that were characteristic of this penumbra of "coarse rusticity". The relentless expansion of Christianity included a process of grooming that was intended to discipline both outward conduct and inner dispositions into conformity with the directives of bishops and other churchmen.[18]

---

[18] Brown (1981) 119-27, discusses the role of saints' cults in the process of socialization implied by the expansion of Christianity: "from late antiquity onwards, the upper-class culture of Europe would always measure itself against the wilderness of a *rusticitas* which it had itself played no small part in creating"

Although Gregory's Latin is usually straightforwardly comprehensible, it also poses many difficulties. Some of the difficulties are due to his style. Gregory tended to be verbose and sometimes lost the pacing and logic of a story or even of a sentence by multiplying subordinate clauses and digressions and by relying on passive verbs, abstract nouns, and clusters of synonyms. His style and manner of presentation often seem closer to the sweeping flow and colloquialism of a sermon or oral discourse than to the concentrated precision of a rewritten narrative. Other difficulties are due to Gregory's inadequate command of Latin. He himself admitted that he did not fully understand the subtleties of Latin syntax and that his prose made him look like a "lumbering ox" [*GC* praef.]. In its failure to understand nuances and details a translation faces the same accusation. But Gregory already provided a defense for both his own writings and subsequent translations. Although he knew he might embarrass himself, his love and fear of Christ compelled him to write. Even better trained writers could benefit from his stories, because at the very least they would find material that they could then rewrite in verse [*GC* praef.]. Modern readers of Gregory too, rather than faulting him for mistakes and obscurities, should instead be grateful for the copious and remarkable information he has provided about late Roman and early Merovingian Gallic society and in particular its contemporary cults of saints. Since the notes are meant merely to provide essential information, identifications, and cross-references to Gregory's other writings, and since in consideration of the potential readership they refer primarily to books and articles written in English or French, they can only hint at the possibilities for subsequent research that Gregory's books of miracles offer.

This translation is based on the great edition of Gregory's books of miracles published by Bruno Krusch in 1885. Previous editions had included one by Thierry Ruinart published in 1699 that was reprinted in *Patrologia Latina* vol.71, col.827-910. In 1860-1862 H.L.Bordier published a text and a French translation of the whole of the *GC*. Modern scholars still rightly use both Ruinart's edition in *PL* and Bordier's text and translation; but it is important to note that the num-

---

(p.124). Mitchell (1987), describes Gregory's saints as "the ethical models of moral leadership."

bering of the chapters in these earlier editions of the *GC* differs from
that in the edition by Krusch, which this translation follows. One
obvious consequence that readers should additionally note is that modern
scholars who do not use Krusch's edition will refer in their own books
and articles to chapter numbers in the *GC* that differ from those here.
The one change from Krusch's edition has to do with the *capitula*.
Gregory provided a list of "headings" for each of his books. Rather
than list them as Gregory (and Krusch) did as a table of contents, this
translation has included them as introductory headings for each chapter.

Krusch was one of the great scholars of Frankish Gaul, and his
editions of the writings of Gregory were a monumental achievement.
In 1890 Max Bonnet published a book on Gregory's Latin that is still
an essential commentary both on Gregory's writings and on Krusch's
edition. In 1920 Krusch collated additional manuscripts that included
readings that are better or more sensible that those in his original edition of Gregory's books of miracles; but unfortunately he did not extend
his collation far enough to include the *GC*.[19] Although between 1937
and 1951 Krusch and W. Levison published a new edition of the *HF*,
there has been little work on the text of the *GC* since Krusch's edition.
A new, properly collated and edited text of all of Gregory's "Books of
Miracles" would be most useful; equipped with a translation and a detailed linguistic and historical commentary in the manner of many of
the wonderful editions in the series "Sources Chrétiennes", it would be
indispensable.

---

[19] B.Krusch, "Appendix. Tomus I. Georgii Florentii Gregorii episcopi
Turonensis libri VIII miraculorum," in *MGH*, SRM 7 (1920) 707-72.

TRANSLATION

Here auspiciously begins the book [entitled] "Glory of the confessors."

It is shameful for a man who is foolish, fraudulent, ignorant, and lazy to undertake what he cannot accomplish. But what am I to do? I forbid concealment of the miracles of the blessed [saints] that I have myself often seen or of the events that obviously happened and that I learned about from an account by trustworthy men and of certain reliability. But because I do not possess the arts of rhetoric or the skill of grammar, I am afraid that when I have begun to write educated men will criticize me : "O ignorant and uneducated man, why do you think to place your name among [those of other] writers? Do you think that this work is to be accepted by experts? Familiarity with style does not support you, nor does any knowledge of literature assist you. You have no useful foundation in literature and you do not know how to distinguish nouns, because often you confuse feminine with masculine, neuter with feminine, and masculine with neuter nouns. Often you do not use in the proper place those prepositions that the authority of distinguished experts fixed for observation; for you substitute accusatives for ablatives and again ablatives for accusatives. Do you think it proper for a lumbering ox to play at some game in the exercise yard or a sluggish donkey to dash among the ranks of a ball game in swift flight? Or can a raven indeed conceal his blackness with the wings of white doves? Can the darkness of tar be changed to the color of flowing milk? Just as it is impossible for these events to happen, so of course you cannot be ranked with other writers."[1]

---

[1] Gregory was a modest man, and he once claimed that he had begun to write his books of history in his "unsophisticated babbling" only because the study of literature had so declined in Gaul that no one was educated enough to take up the task [*HF* praef.]. In fact, his own familiarity with classical literature was limited: see Bonnet (1890) 48-53, Kurth (1919) I:1-29, and especially Riché (1976) 177-210, for the wider context of the survival of classical culture in

But I will nevertheless respond to these criticisms and say: "I am doing [the same] task as you, and by my [literary] incompetence I will engage your wisdom. For I think that these writings will offer you one benefit: what I describe unskillfully and briefly in an obscure style, you will amplify in verse standing clearly and sumptuously on longer pages."

In a first book [*GM*] I therefore included some of the miracles of the Lord, the holy apostles, and the other martyrs. These miracles had been unknown until now, [but] God deigned to increase them daily to strengthen the faith of believers. For it was surely improper that they disappear from memory. In a second book [*VJ*] I wrote about the miracles of St Julian. [I wrote] four books [*VM* 1-4] about the miracles of St Martin, and a seventh [*VP*] about the life of some blessed [saints]. I am writing this eighth book about the miracles of the confessors. I specifically request of the reader that, because no familiarity with style and no facility with words assist me (as I have often admitted), he graciously grant indulgence to my boldness. Worldly arrogance does not compel me to write; rather, embarrassment forces me to be silent, but love and fear of Christ compel me to repay [my gratitude]. Since I began the first book with miracles of the Lord, I wish to provide for this book an introduction about the miracles of the holy angels.

1. The miracles of angels.

While I was living in the territory of Clermont, a trustworthy man talked with me; I know that he told the truth because I knew that what he said had certainly happened. He said that he gave orders that a drink be brewed for the reapers from grain soaked and boiled in water. [The historian] Orosius wrote that this brew was called "caelia" because of the cooking.[2] The man delayed in the city. When the drink had been

----

southern and central Gaul. Near the end of his life Gregory conceded that his books might be rewritten into verse, so long as they were kept intact [*HF* X.31]. He also exchanged some correspondence with his friend the poet Fortunatus about the possibility of having some of his writings versified [see *GC* 22].

[2] In the early fifth century the Spanish historian Orosius had composed a polemical "History against the pagans" that surveyed both Roman history and the history of the church. Gregory found Orosius' survey useful for information about past events [*HF* I praef., II praef., V praef.]; here he referred to a passage from Orosius, *Historiae adversum paganos* V.7, that described the concoction of

prepared and stored in a container, the servants, as is characteristic, drank most of it and left only a little for the intentions of the lord. The lord relied upon his instructions and ordered the reapers to be invited, so that when he returned from the city he might find them cutting his corn. This was done, and about seventy workers were gathered in the cornfield. The lord of the estate arrived and inspected the quality and the quantity of the drink; but he found only a little bit. The lord was embarrassed because he determined that no more than five measures were left.[3] Thinking that this had been done to shame him, so that there would not be enough drink for the workers, he was uncertain what to do or where to turn. Finally, with the inspiration of the Lord he turned to the container and piously recited over its mouth the names of the holy angels that the sacred readings taught. He prayed that their power deign to transform this pittance into an abundance, so that the workers would not lack something to drink. [What happened next is] extraordinary to report! Throughout the entire day drinkers never lacked [drink] drawn from this container. Until nightfall ended work, drink was served in abundance to everyone.

2. St Hilary, bishop of Poitiers.

In the fourth year of his exile the most blessed Hilary returned to his own city [of Poitiers] and, after completing the passage of his [life's] good work, migrated to the Lord. Many miracles are said to be shown at his blessed tomb, which the book of his life has recorded. Two lepers were also cleansed in the same place.[4]

_____

some sort of beer: ed. C.Zangemeister, *CSEL* 5 (1882) 294-5, and trans. I.W.Raymond, *Seven books of history against the pagans. The apology of Paulus Orosius* (New York, 1936) 220, with Weidemann (1982) II:369.

[3] Five *modii*, about forty-six quarts: see Weidemann (1982) II:342-3.

[4] Hilary (Helarius or Hilarius) served as bishop of Poitiers from c.350 until 367 or 368. He distinguished himself by his opposition to Arianism: see Griffe (1964-1966) I:218-70. The "book of his life" to which Gregory referred was probably the *Vita S. Hilarii* written by Fortunatus: ed. B.Krusch, *MGH*, AA 4.2 (1885) 1-7. But the miracle of the two lepers was recorded in Fortunatus, *Liber de virtutibus S. Hilarii* 11-14: ed. B.Krusch, o.c. 8-9. Fortunatus dedicated both books to bishop Pascentius of Poitiers. Since Pascentius' successor, Maroveus, was already bishop of Poitiers by the time Radegund acquired relics of the True Cross in 568-569 [*GC* 104], Fortunatus must have composed these books soon after his arrival in Gaul in 566: see Meyer (1901) 23, and Brennan (1985) 61-2.

In the territory of Javols there was a mountain named after Hilary that contained a large lake. At a fixed time a crowd of rustics went there and, as if offering libations to the lake, threw [into it] linen cloths and garments that served men as clothing. Some [threw] pelts of wool, many [threw] models of cheese and wax and bread as well as various [other] objects, each according to his own means, that I think would take too long to enumerate. They came with their wagons; they brought food and drink, sacrificed animals, and feasted for three days. But before they were due to leave on the fourth day, a violent storm approached them with thunder and lightning. The heavy rainfall and hailstones fell with such force that each person thought he would not escape. Every year this happened this way, but these foolish people were tied up in their mistake. Much later a cleric from that city [of Javols] became bishop and went to the place. He preached to the crowds that they should cease this behavior lest they be consumed by the wrath of heaven. But their coarse rusticity rejected his preaching. Then, with the inspiration of the Divinity this bishop of God built a church in honor of the blessed Hilary of Poitiers at a distance from the banks of the lake. He placed relics of Hilary in the church and said to the people: "Do not, my sons, do not sin before God! For there is [to be] no religious piety to a lake. Do not stain your hearts with these empty rituals, but rather acknowledge God and direct your devotion to his friends. Respect St Hilary, a bishop of God whose relics are located here. For he can serve as your intercessor [for] the mercy of the Lord." The men were stung in their hearts and converted. They left the lake and brought everything they usually threw into it to the holy church. So they were freed from the mistake that had bound them. Next the storm was banned from the place. After the relics of the blessed confessor were placed there, the storm never again threatened this festival of God.[5]

---

[5] This lake may have been the lake of Saint-Andéol, in the Aubrac mountains: see Vieillard-Troiekouroff (1976) 246. The bishop who opposed these pagan sacrifices may have been Hilarius (or Hilarus), bishop of Javols in the early sixth century; if so, then he was here honoring his namesake: see Duchesne (1894-1915) II:54-5.

3. St Eusebius, bishop of Vercelli.

Bishop Eusebius of Vercelli was a great supporter of Hilary against heresies.[6] He shows that he is still alive after his burial by his current miracles. For although many ill people are cured on his anniversary day, possessed people dance throughout the entire church in violent spins and believe that they are afflicted with powerful torments. They leap in the air and with their hands strike and break the lamps that are burning as lights. Once they are soaked with the oil from a lamp, immediately the demon leaves and the people are cleansed. Then the congregation knows that the number of ill people who have been healed matches the number of lamps that it sees are broken. The saint guards everything that his church owns with such a devout protection, lest someone steal something from it. For you might see that even among unjust enemies no one touches the herds of cattle, horses, and sheep when the voice has sounded: "These belong to the confessor Eusebius."

My mother placed relics of this saint in the oratory of her own house.[7] One day during winter it happened that she was enjoying a conversation during the long night and sat for a long time before the fireplace, which was arranged with a large pile of logs. When the rest of the household went to sleep, she arose and laid herself on a bed not far from this fire. While everyone was asleep, sparks of fire jumped to the rafters. One of the rafters was set on fire and began to scatter flames widely. But I believe that because of the power of St Eusebius, whose relics were nearby, the flame was curved and twisted from above, contrary to nature. The fire did not spread to the roof, as is common, but flowed down, so that you might think that pelts of wool, not flames,

---

[6] Eusebius was bishop of Vercelli in the middle of the fourth century. Gregory considered Hilary and Eusebius as important representatives of orthodox catholic theology and once cited their dual authority in opposition to the idiosyncratic theological views of king Chilperic [*HF* V.44].

[7] The location of this house is uncertain. Gregory occasionally visited his mother "in terretorium Cavellonensis urbis" [*VM* 3.60]. Given Gregory's erratic spelling, it is not obvious what city he meant here. Some have identified this city as Cabillonum, i.e. Chalon-sur-Saône: see Pietri (1983) 253 n.40. This seems the most plausible identification; note that Gregory's mother once seems to have accompanied him to visit a shrine in Chalon-sur-Saône [*GC* 84]. But others have identified the city as Cabellio, i.e. Cavaillon, and then located the oratory at Cabrières: see Vieillard-Troiekouroff (1976) 73, 76.

were hanging from the beam. Even though the blazing fire spread over the beam, it did not burn it until my mother awoke, called her servants, and extinguished the fire by throwing water on it. If the power of the blessed saint had been lacking, the entire house could easily have been burned by this fire while everyone was asleep.

4. St Martin, bishop of Tours, and the tomb of St Catianus.

I have learned from current opinion that bishop Catianus was sent by the Roman bishops to Tours and was entrusted as the first bishop of Tours.[8] Once when the blessed Martin came to pray at his tomb, he poured out his requests, recited the verses [of psalms], and said: "Bless me, man of God." As he said this, a voice was heard descending to him. It said: "Servant of God, I request that you bless me." After Martin prayed again, he left. Those who were present at the time were surprised and said that he who had once summoned Lazarus from his tomb was now dwelling in Martin.[9]

---

[8] On the basis of the chronology in a "History of the suffering of the martyr St Saturninus" and other unspecified evidence, Gregory elsewhere claimed that seven men had been consecrated as bishops and sent to preach in Gaul during the middle of the third century [*HF* I.30]: see Levillain (1927). These seven missionaries included (in Gregory's order) Catianus (or Gatianus) of Tours, Trophimus of Arles, Paulus of Narbonne, Saturninus of Toulouse [*GM* 47], Dionysius of Paris [*GM* 71], Stremonius of Clermont [*GC* 29], and Martialis of Limoges [*GC* 27]. The accuracy of this chronology for Catianus is suspect, however, since Martin, who became bishop in 371, was according to Gregory only the third bishop of Tours [*HF* X.31]. Gregory resolved the discrepancy by stating that the see was vacant for thirty-seven years after Catianus' episcopacy [*HF* X.31]: see Pietri (1983) 17-33.

[9] In this and subsequent chapters Gregory included some apparently apocryphal legends about Martin of Tours. The most important sources for information about what men believed to have been the historical Martin were the writings of Sulpicius Severus, a younger contemporary of Martin who wrote a *Vita* and *Dialogi* about him: ed. C.Halm, *CSEL* 1 (1866), and trans. A.Roberts, NPNF 2nd series, 11 (reprinted 1973), with Stancliffe (1983). Gregory had read Sulpicius' books [*VM* 1.1, *GC* 20]; but neither Sulpicius nor other early writers had mentioned these particular legends, many of which either justified the potency of certain objects and relics or explained the importance of certain shrines. Yet Gregory showed no hesitation or uncertainty about including the legends. Sulpicius had already admitted that he had omitted information about Martin: see his *Vita Martini* 1.7-9, 26.1, and *Dialogi* II.14.8, ed. Halm, o.c.

5. The same saint and the tomb of the virgin Vitalina.

Often I have heard old men saying that a similar event happened at
Artonne, a village in the territory of Clermont. A nun named Vitalina
was buried in this place. The blessed Martin came to her tomb and
gave a greeting. But she requested that he might deign to bless her.
After they prayed, the blessed man turned and said: "Holy virgin, tell
me, have you already deserved [to be in] the presence of the Lord?" She
said: "One misfortune that seemed insignificant in the world is an
obstacle for me. On the [Good] Friday when we know that the redeemer
of the world suffered, I washed my face in water." As the blessed confessor left the tomb of the virgin, he said to his companions: "Woe to
us, who live in this world! If this virgin who was dedicated to Christ
incurred this obstacle because she washed her face on [Good] Friday,
what are we to do, whom a deceitful world everyday persuades to
commit sins?" In that village the blessed man performed many deeds
that I think it would take too long to include.[10]

When the man of God left the village of Artonne, he journeyed to
Clermont. The senators of that city, who in that place were then distinguished by a pedigree of Roman nobility, heard that the holy man
was approaching the city. In order to meet him they went out with
horsemen, coaches, chariots, and wagons. Martin was riding a donkey
and seated on a very plain saddle. When he came to the summit of a
ridge at Saint-Bonnet from which the location of the village of Riom
was visible, he saw these people approaching him in this procession.
He said: "What do these people who are approaching us with this

---

111, 136, 198, and trans. Roberts, o.c. 4, 16, 46. Gregory in contrast emphasized that he would not do likewise [*GC* 6]; and he furthermore claimed to
possess "huge volumes" cataloguing the miracles of bishop Martin [*HF* II.1].
Due to the circulation of these additional legends and their revised contemporary
meanings and functions, the image of St Martin current in the later sixth century
was therefore a transformation of earlier images of the saint: see Fontaine
(1976), and Van Dam (1988a).

[10] Although contemporary councils prohibited people from working and
various other activities on Sundays and festival days in honor of saints,
Gregory's miracle stories provide many examples of people who "insulted" these
days [*HF* X.30] and became ill or suffered disaster [cf. *GC* 80, 97]: see Wood
(1979) 62-5, and Van Dam (1985) 285-8.

magnificence intend for themselves?" A man who had arrived earlier replied: "The senators of Clermont are coming to meet you." Martin said to him: "It is not my [intention] to enter their city with this ostentatious parade." Immediately he turned the bridle of the donkey around and began to depart on the road by which he had come. But the men [of Clermont] followed him and humbly begged that he visit their city; they said: "We have heard about the reputation of your holiness. For there are many ill people whom you ought to visit." Although they were unable to convince him, Martin laid his hands on the ill people who had come and restored them to health. He returned to the village of Artonne. Even now there is a railing around the spot where the saint is said to have stood.[11]

Afterwards Martin went to the tomb of the virgin and said: "Vitalina, blessed sister, rejoice now, because after three days you will be presented to the majesty of the Lord." Then he left that place. Many then saw the virgin in a vision; she offered them the benefits they sought and announced the day of her death on which her memory would be celebrated. This must be understood in no other way than that she had deserved [to be in] the presence of the Lord's majesty because of the plea of the blessed bishop and could then make these announcements.

Once after the vigils had been celebrated in her honor Eulalius, the archpriest of the place, invited the clerics to a meal. But another priest named Edatius had prepared food for widows and other poor people. One lacked fish, the other some good wine. In a dream the virgin advised a fisherman to bring a supply of fish to the archpriest. The fisherman rose from his bed and discovered in his weir a huge pike

---

[11] Although Gregory had probably heard this story about Martin's failure to visit Clermont from "old men", it had special significance for him after he became bishop of Tours in 573. During an attempt to oust Gregory in 580 a rival claimed to be "cleansing" Tours of "those people from Clermont." Gregory insisted that he was not an interloper at Tours and responded by pointing out that most of the preceding bishops of Tours had been members of his family [*HF* V.49]. This particular miracle story would also have been useful for his case, since it neatly explained why the patron saint of his own episcopal see had never visited the city of which he was a native son: excessive veneration, not indifference or lack of respect, had caused Martin to turn back from Clermont.

which he brought where he had been ordered. Likewise the virgin appeared in a vision to the priest Edatius and said: "Go, and you will find a small gold coin beneath a tree in the courtyard. After presenting the gold coin you will purchase wine worthy of a meal for the poor." The priest mentioned what he had seen to no one; but he went out, looked, and found [the gold coin]. He bought wine and nourished the poor of Christ. In this way the power of the virgin appeared to both men and enriched both with the commodities that were lacking.

6. The stone on which the saint [Martin] sat.

Martin performed many deeds in this world, most of which the writers of his life have omitted. For they tried to anticipate the disdain of critics, lest they not be believed by those who often wish to attack the holiness of good men with their poisonous tongues. But I who, even though unworthy, every day see his miracles at his tomb—for ill people, not healthy people, have need of a doctor [cf. Matthew 9:12, Mark 2:17]—I think it ridiculous if I am silent about those events that I have learned he obviously did in the past. But if there is still someone who does not believe and is so envious that he does not accept these facts, let him go the the church [of St Martin at Tours]. Everyday he will see both new miracles and repetition of what happened long ago. I have already written a third book about the deeds of Martin [*VM* 3]. But lest this book [the *GC*] be deprived of his miracles, I have decided to include in it some of the stories that are clearly known to me; for there are many events that are still unknown, as I have often stated.

In the church mentioned above that the believers built in his honor there is still a stone on which the blessed man is said to have sat. Many years later a priest named Leo moved the holy stone from its spot in order to set down his own tomb. Immediately he returned to his house with a tremor, was struck by a fever, and died on the third day. It was clear that bishop Martin had been insulted. I recall that this happened during my lifetime.[12]

---

[12] Bishop Perpetuus had built this church of St Martin outside Tours probably during the 460s and early 470s, although subsequent bishops (including Gregory) modified and restored it: see Vieillard-Troiekouroff (1976) 311-24, Pietri (1983) 372-405, and Van Dam (1985) 230-55. Many of the miracles that Gregory recorded in his *VM* happened in or near this church.

7. The tree that was raised up.

In Neuillé-le-Lierre, a village in the territory of Tours, there was a tree that fell over during a strong wind and blocked the public road. When the blessed Martin was travelling on this road and noted that the way was blocked by this fallen tree, he was moved by pity. He made the sign of the cross over the tree and raised it up. Still today this tree is seen to stand up straight next to the road. But even though it is dead because it has been stripped of its bark, it always lives to the honor of this man of God. Many people have faithfully scraped at its bark, and after they have taken and dissolved the bark in water, soon they received a medicine. I myself have seen this tree standing erect.

8. The oratory on an estate at Martigny.

Near a village in the territory of Tours there was an oratory situated in the villa of Martigny. It was commonly reported that Martin had often prayed in this oratory. Whenever the opportunity arose for abbot Guntharius, while he was head of his community of monks, to travel on the road that passed not far from this oratory, he prayed before travelling on. After he became bishop [of Tours], he passed by on this road and came to the oratory, but he hesitated to dismount to pray in this place. Immediately his horse turned his head toward the oratory and stood in the middle of the road. Guntharius kicked the horse with his feet, whipped it, and spurred it on; but like a bronze [statue] it was not moved. Then the bishop realized that it was held by divine power. He dismounted, prayed, remounted his horse, and travelled on. O horse, if the Lord would open your mouth as he once did for a donkey [cf. Numbers 22:28-30], I wish that you would say what was so spectacular that you did not move. What was so attractive that you stared at the door of the shrine? What was so frightening that you compelled your rider to pray? Without doubt you would shout in a louder voice that you witnessed the splendor of Martin and did not dare to move until your master had performed his usual greeting.[13]

[13] Guntharius was abbot of the monastery of St Venantius [GC 15] before serving as bishop of Tours from 552 until 555. Frankish kings often used him as an envoy; but by the end of his episcopacy he was an alcoholic [HF X.31].

9. The oil from the tomb [of St Martin].

Aredius, a priest from Limoges and a man of the highest goodness and holiness, was once sitting with me in his cell.[14] I began to ask whether any miracles had been displayed in the oratory where he had placed relics of the blessed bishop [Martin]. Aredius said that he had once visited Tours during the episcopacy of the blessed Eufronius.[15] After staying there a long time, he took away a vial full of oil from the tomb of the holy bishop [Martin]. He returned home. Worn out by the journey he sat down and recounted the efforts of the trip to his mother; suddenly he was struck so hard by a piercing pain that he could scarcely draw a breath. But he turned to the oratory in which relics of the blessed bishop were kept, and after spending the night in vigils at daybreak he smeared the spot of his pain with the oil that he had brought. The pain lessened, and he recovered. Later a man presented his hand that had swelled up after being pierced by a thorn; as soon as it was smeared with oil, it was restored to health. A woman who had lost her senses and was thought to possess a demon at certain hours was healed after being touched by this oil. Another abbot who [lived] next to this shrine touched the eyes of a blind man with this oil; the blind man immediately recovered his sight. Since the oil had restored many possessed people to health, he placed some of it on the head of one man who possessed, I think, a more hideous demon. Immediately the man expelled the demon in a blast of air from his bowels. A demon descended upon another man in the nail of his thumb. When he saw this, the priest [Aredius] poured oil over the finger. Soon the skin broke,

[14] Gregory also wrote a separate account of the miracles and the death of Aredius, an abbot at Limoges whom Gregory greatly admired and who died in 591 [*HF* X.29]. With the support of his mother Pelagia [*GC* 102] Aredius had founded a monastery at Saint-Yrieix, in the oratory of which he kept relics of St Martin [*HF* VIII.15]: see Vieillard-Troiekouroff (1976) 277-8. Aredius often visited Tours [*VM* 2.39, 3.24, 4.6], and served as an informant for Gregory [*GM* 36, 41, *VJ* 41-5, *VP* 17 praef.]. A *Vita* of Aredius survives, composed probably during the Carolingian period: ed. B.Krusch, *MGH*, SRM 3 (1896) 581-609.

[15] Eufronius (or Euphronius) served as bishop of Tours from 556 until 573 [*HF* X.31]. When he became bishop, king Chlothar noted that his was one of the foremost families in Gaul [*HF* IV.15]. Gregory could feel justifiably proud, since Eufronius was his mother's cousin. Gregory also visited Tours while Eufronius was bishop [*VM* 1.32].

blood flowed, and the demon left. Aredius told these stories about the oil.

10. A cluster [of grapes] from the vine that he planted, and the wax from his tomb.

Aredius added a story about a cluster [of grapes] from the vine that St Martin had planted. After picking a cluster Aredius put it in a vial that he filled with water. A bit later a man came to him. The man's mouth was swollen from an infected pustule, and his face and his puffed-up eyes were obstructed with excessive poison. Once his mouth had been soaked with water from the vial with the cluster, the pimple disappeared and the swelling and the pain completely vanished. Aredius always claimed that the grapes from the cluster remained fresh in this water still four years later. He added a story about the wax [of candles] that he brought from the tomb [of St Martin]. A deaf and dumb woman who, I think, possessed a demon came to him. He put some of this wax in her ear. When she returned the next day, she thanked the priest for the health she had recovered.

11. His miracles shown at Tonnerre.

A priest who was crippled in his foot lived in the territory of the village of Tonnerre, which is joined to Langres. As he was travelling along the road that led to the cathedral of God, he met an old man accompanied by a young boy, both of whom were clerics. After they greeted each other, the old man said to the priest: "Do you wish to be cured?" The priest replied: "What more do men wish to have than that they might live healthy in body?" The old man made the sign of the cross over the priest's knee and said to him: "In the name of our Lord Jesus Christ, stretch out your foot." Immediately the priest stretched out his foot and bent it back cured. After thanking them the priest began to walk on to where he was going. The young boy who was with the old man called him and said: "Priest, do you know who this man is who has restored you to health?" The priest said: "I do not know." The young boy replied: "St Martin, bishop of Tours, has himself restored you to health with his power. Without delay construct an oratory on the spot where you saw the saint standing. If you do what I say, the oratory will benefit people." The priest immediately constructed an oratory on the same spot. In it many paralytics recently deserved to receive mobility, and blind people deserved to receive their sight.[16]

12. His monastery in Spain.

I have learned of something that recently happened in Spain. When king Leovigild marched against his own son, his army (as often happens) severely damaged the holy shrines. Between Sagunto and Cartagena there was a monastery of St Martin. When the monks heard that this army was intending to approach their locale, they fled, abandoned their old abbot, and went to an island in the [Mediterranean] sea. The Goths arrived and destroyed the possessions of the monastery that had been left without any guard; they also found the abbot, who was bent over from old age but upright in his holiness. One of the Goths drew his sword to cut off the abbot's head, but he fell over backwards and exhaled his spirit. As soon as the other Goths saw this, they were terrified with fear and fled. When the news was announced to the king, he issued a public order that everything that had been stolen was to be returned to the monastery.[17]

[16] The location of this oratory is uncertain: see Vieillard-Troiekouroff (1976) 356. Equally uncertain is the commonness of young boys serving as minor clerics; note the career of the priest Cato of Clermont, who had perhaps become a lector at age ten [*HF* IV.6]: see Beck (1950) 52-3, and Riché (1976) 282-5.

[17] Leovigild ruled as sole king of the Visigoths in Spain from 571 or 573 until 586 [*HF* IV.38, VIII.46]. His son Hermenegild married a daughter of the Frankish king Sigibert in 579 and converted from Arian to catholic Christianity [*HF* V.38]. According to Gregory, his conversion precipitated a civil war; but in 583 his father defeated him at Seville, and in 584 he took his son captive and sent him into exile, where Hermenegild was killed the next year [*HF* VI.43, VIII.28]. In fact, it is more likely that this revolt marked a reaction against Leovigild's attempts to impose a dominant centralized monarchy and that Hermenegild converted only after the outbreak of the rebellion: see Collins (1980) and (1983) 45-53. The cult of St Martin was particularly prominent in Galicia, a region in northwestern Spain occupied by the Sueves, where bishop Martin of Braga had promoted it in the mid-sixth century before his death in 580 [*HF* V.37, *VM* 1.11, 4.7]. Leovigild's generosity to this monastery of St Martin may have been part of his policy of trying to win support from catholic Christians during the civil war; in 585 he incorporated Galicia into his kingdom [*HF* VIII.35]: see Thompson (1969) 64-91.

✗

13. The heretic who wished to restore a man's sight.

When the aforementioned king [Leovigild] heard of the miracles that were worked through the servants of God who belonged to our [catholic] faith, he summoned one of his own [Arian] bishops and in secret said to him: "Why do you, in accordance with your faith, not display miracles to the people just like those who call themselves Christians?" The bishop said to him: "Often I have restored sight to the blind and hearing to the deaf. I am now able to accomplish these things that you suggest." The bishop summoned one of the heretics and said to him in private: "Take these forty gold pieces, close your eyes, and sit down in a place where I pass by. When I pass by with the king, cry out loudly that I might restore your lost sight by means of my faith." The man took the money and did what had been ordered of him. The new Cyrila walked at the right hand of the king, surrounded by a crowd of heretics. The man who had been blinded by the money shouted that he might recover [sight in] his eyes by the faith of the bishop. With great arrogance the bishop placed his hands over the man's eyes and said: "In accordance with my faith, let this happen for you." As he said this, the man's eyes were closed up so painfully that not only did he lose his sight but he also confessed the deceit that he had contrived for the sake of greediness.[18]

14. The argument of a heretic with a catholic.

Another trustworthy man reported that he had seen a Christian struggling with a heretic on behalf of our faith. After they had argued for a long time over the divine Scriptures, the heretic could not be persuaded to know the truth. Then the man of our religion said: "If the

[18] Cyrila was the leading Arian bishop in the kingdom of the Vandals in North Africa during the early 480s: see Mandouze (1982) 260-2. His attempt to perform a miracle by restoring sight to a man who feigned blindness was equally unsuccessful; Gregory's account of Cyrila was similar to the story in this chapter, although longer and more detailed [*HF* II.3]. Gregory thought that king Leovigild may have converted to catholic Christianity before his death [*HF* VIII.46]. In fact, Reccared, his son and successor, converted in 587 after first, according to Gregory, reminding the Arian bishops of this particular example of their failure to work miracles [*HF* IX.15]. The Council of Toledo in 589 ratified and publicized the imposition of catholic Christianity in Visigothic Spain: see Thompson (1969) 94-109, and Collins (1983) 53-8.

evidence of the sacred Scriptures does not convince you to believe, then
recognize the power of our indivisible Trinity in miracles. I have a
gold ring on my finger; I will toss it into a fire, and you pick it up
when it is glowing hot." He tossed the ring among the coals and
allowed it to become so red-hot that it seemed to resemble the coals.
He turned to the heretic and said: "If your exposition is true, take the
ring from the fire." When the heretic was reluctant, the man said:
"God, immeasurable Trinity, reveal whether I believe something that is
unworthy of you. For indeed, if my faith is correct, let these fierce
flames not have power over me." And after he took the ring from the
fire he held it for a long time in his hand but was not harmed. More
importantly, the heretic was upset, and this man strengthened the other
catholics with the intensity of his own faith. Enough on this matter.

15. Abbot Venantius.

Abbot Venantius is buried not far from the church of the blessed
Martin [at Tours].[19] Venantius was a man of outstanding holiness who,
while alive, offered assistance to many ill people. At the end of his
time he migrated from this world, but he continually demonstrates
through his miracles that he lives in eternity. For if someone who has
developed chilling fevers prays and keeps vigils for one night at his
tomb, soon the attack of fever subsides and he receives a cure. Among
the other [miracles] that I either witnessed or heard of that happened
there, I saw a woman who had been healed after being afflicted by a
quartan fever. For a long time she had been hampered by this affliction
and was unable to eat or sleep; she had so deteriorated in her whole body
that she scarcely possessed the breath of life. She spent the night at the
tomb of Venantius crying and praying and remained motionless until
daybreak. At dawn she fell asleep. When awakened, she felt no pain
and left with her health. I have written a *Vita* of this saint.

16. St Papula.

Papula was a committed ascetic who often demanded of her parents
that she be admitted to a convent of nuns, because she was not able to

---

[19] Gregory's longer account of Venantius was *VP* 16. Venantius had broken
off his engagement to join a monastery at Tours, where he eventually served as
abbot until his death in the later fifth century.

serve God in the house of her parents [where she was] distracted by the
concerns of this world. Her parents loved her and did not want her to be
separated from them. So she cut the hair on her head, put on the
clothes of a man, journeyed to the diocese of Tours, and enrolled herself
in a community of monks. There she led a life of fasting and praying
and was noted for her many miracles. For Papula was like a man
among men, and no one knew of her gender. Her parents looked for her
but could never find her. Meanwhile the abbot of the monastery that
she had joined died. Because of her constant miracles the monks selected her [as abbot], although they did not know of her gender. With
all her strength Papula rejected the office. Although she lived in the
monastery for thirty years, no one knew what she was. But three days
before she migrated from this world, she revealed her secret to the
monks. When she died, she was washed by other women and buried.
Through her many miracles she reveals that she is a servant of God.
For often people suffering from chills and other illnesses are restored to
their health at her tomb.[20]

17. The lid of a certain tomb.

In another district of Tours a tomb was situated among thorn-
bushes and brambles. It was said that a bishop was buried in this
tomb, but they did not know his name. It happened that the son of a
poor man died. After the boy was buried, the poor man did not find a
cover for his sarcophagus; so he went to this spot and took the lid from
this tomb. The lid was so huge that three yoke of oxen dragged it. By
stealing from the tomb of another man the poor man covered the body
of his son. But once he had done this, he became deaf, mute, blind, and
crippled. For almost an entire year he suffered from this distress. Then
a bishop appeared to him in a dream and said: "What evil, o man, have
I inflicted upon you and your family because you have uncovered me by
removing the lid of my tomb? Go now if you wish to be made
healthy, and order that this lid be quickly restored. If you do not do

---

[20] Papula (or Papola) is otherwise unknown. The literary motif, although
not necessarily the occurrence, of holy women entering monasteries as
transvestites was common in both western and eastern medieval literature: see
Anson (1974), Patlagean (1976), and the sophisticated and powerful analysis of
Bynum (1987) 277-96.

this, you will die immediately. For I am bishop Benignus, who came
as a foreigner to this city." The man nodded to his servants and went to
his son's grave. He lifted the stone lid and put it on a wagon. Once he
brought it and restored it to the tomb [of the bishop], he was immediately healed. On its return the stone lid was so light that two oxen
could haul back what three yoke of oxen had removed.[21]

18. The tombs of two virgins.

Within the territory of Tours there was a small hill that was
covered with briers and brambles and wild vines. The hill was so
densely entwined in vines that scarcely anyone could climb it. Rumor
reported that two virgins who had been dedicated to God were buried in
this place. During the vigils before festival days believers often saw a
light burning there by the power of God. One brave man trusted in the
impulse of his heart and did not fear to approach the place during a dark
night. He saw a candle shining with the vast light of a marvelous
brightness. After watching it for a long time, he left and told others
what he had seen. Then the virgins revealed themselves to one of the
local inhabitants in a dream. They explained that they had been buried
there and that without a shelter they could not endure any longer the
damage from storms. But if this man wished to be of use to them, then
he should cut down the thorn-bushes and build a roof over their tombs.
When the man awoke, his other concerns overwhelmed him and he
forgot what he had seen. On another night the virgins appeared to him
again and horribly threatened him with a menacing scowl that he would
migrate from this world during the current year if he did not cover the
place. The man was terrified by this dream. He took his axe, chopped
down the thicket, and exposed the tombs. He found large drops of
candle wax that were fragrant with the scent of nectar, similar to frank-
incense. He hitched oxen to a wagon, collected stones, and built an
oratory during the summer.

When it was completed, he invited the blessed Eufronius, who was
then bishop in the cathedral of Tours, to bless it. But Eufronius was
wearied by old age and excused himself from going; he said: "My son,
you see that I am an old man and that a winter that is more harsh than

---

[21] This bishop Benignus is otherwise unknown; his tomb was at Saint-
Branchs: see Vieillard-Troiekouroff (1976) 248-9.

usual bothers me. Rains are falling, the winds are blowing everything in a whirl, rivers are high, and the roads are soaked from the frequent rains and almost turned into mud. It is not now appropriate for my old age to undertake these journeys." The man listened to these excuses and left the sight of the bishop, feeling very sad as he departed. But when the bishop relaxed his limbs for a rest, he saw the two virgins standing by him. The older of the two had a sad look and began to speak: "Why do we not deserve your favor, most blessed bishop? What misfortune have we brought upon the region entrusted to you by God? Why do you disdain us? Why do you hesitate to come to consecrate the place that this faithful man has constructed for us? Come now, we beg in the name of the omnipotent God whose servants we are." After she said this, her cheeks became damp with the tears that appeared. The old man awoke, called the superintendent of the church house, and said: "I have sinned by not going with that man. Behold, I saw the two virgins who rebuked me for this reason; I am afraid of committing an offense against God if I delay going there." As Eufronius travelled along the road, he hurried on his way. During his journey the rainstorm stopped and the harsh violence of the winds died down. After successfully completing his trip Eufronius blessed the place and then returned in peace. For he often recalled the appearance and the features of the virgins. He said that one was taller while the other was smaller in size but not in merit, and that both were whiter than snow. He announced that one was Maura and the other Britta and said that he had learned these names from their own mouths.[22]

19. What St Eufronius predicted about king Charibert.

Although many people often urged Bishop Eufronius that he ought to meet with king Charibert, he contrived delays and hesitated to go. Finally he was convinced by his servants and said: "Go, prepare for a journey, so that we might meet with the king whom we will not see." Then supplies were loaded on wagons and horses were readied for the journey. When the moment for him to set out on the road was at hand, he said: "The wagons are to be turned around, and the horses are to be

[22] St Maura and St Britta are otherwise unknown; this oratory over their tombs was located at Sainte-Maure: see Vieillard-Troiekouroff (1976) 279-80. Eufronius was bishop of Tours from 556 until 573 [see note to *GC* 9].

unsaddled. We are not making this trip now." His servants asked what
the joke was, so that he so easily undid what he had already ordered to
be prepared with great urgency. In private Eufronius said: "The ruler to
whom you force me to journey has died; if we were to go, we would
not find him alive." The men who heard this remark were amazed; they
noted the day and quietly remembered the words of the saint. Men came
from Paris and announced that the king had died at the very hour when
the bishop ordered the wagons to be recalled from the journey.[23]

20. The dedication of my oratory.

With regard to my oratory, in which are located relics of the martyr
St Saturninus, bishop Martin, the confessor Illidius, and other saints, it
will not be out of place to narrate some stories for the instruction of
believers. [I will tell] how the power of the blessed Martin displayed
itself in a revelation, so that many saw that fearsome ball of fire that
once was visible to a few as it rose from Martin while he was celebrating mass and burst from the top of his head. Under the guidance of
the inspiration of divine piety my heart decided that I should faithfully
dedicate for the task of praying the very beautiful room that St Eufronius had used as a storeroom. The room was carefully arranged and the
altar placed in the usual spot. One night I kept vigils in the holy
church [of St Martin]; at dawn I went to the oratory and sanctified the
altar I had set up. I returned to the church and with the accompaniment
of crosses and burning candles formally transferred the holy relics of
Martin along with those of the martyrs Saturninus and Julian and of the
blessed Illidius. A large group of clerics and deacons dressed in white
was present, as well as the illustrious order of distinguished citizens and
a large crowd of people of the next rank. After I lifted and carried the
holy relics that were [placed] in wooden coffers and adorned in shrouds, I
came to the door of the oratory. As I entered, suddenly a frightening
flash filled the room, so that the eyes of the bystanders were closed out
of fear and because of the great brightness. The flash, so to speak,
flared about through the entire oratory and made me very afraid. No one
could know what this was, although everyone was prostrate with fear
and lay on the ground. I said: "Do not be afraid. For it is the power of

---

[23] King Charibert died in 567 [*HF* IV.45]; a wise woman had also predicted
the hour, day, and year of his death [*HF* V.14].

the saints that you see. In particular remember the book about the life of the blessed Martin and recall how a ball of fire rose from his head as he recited the sacred words [of the liturgy] and how it was seen to ascend all the way to heaven. Therefore, do not be afraid, but believe that he and the other saints have visited us." Then we set aside our fear and praised God by saying: "Blessed is he who comes in the name of the Lord; the Lord is God and he has given us light" [Psalm 118:26-27].

That earlier miracle was seen by only a few people, but this one appeared to all the people. In that earlier miracle there was evidence of power, but in this one there was a reinforcement of grace. That earlier miracle was kept secret to avoid ostentation, but this one was made manifest to everyone for glorification. Then the celebration of the festival was being faithfully proclaimed to the Lord; in this case the new oratory that would contribute to the praise of the Lord was being consecrated by the display of holy relics. Therefore we must faithfully ask and pray, as is proper, that he [Martin] who often raised on high the vows of his prayer through this sacred fire now look upon this congregation. For both when I wrote about the monk who was praying and when I revealed that abbot Brachio had seen the fire rise from the relics of saints, I think that this fire is a mystical one, because it enlightens but does not burn. But it can neither emerge nor ever appear to anyone without the grace of the divine majesty.[24]

21. The tomb of St Sollemnis.

I have already written some [stories] about Tours. But since I recently visited the tomb of St Sollemnis, I cannot be silent about what [happened] at the monastery at Luynes, which is built on the summit of

---

[24] Gregory dedicated this new oratory within a year after he became bishop at Tours [*VP* 2.3]. Three of these saints whose relics he transferred had special significance for him personally. St Martin was the patron saint of his new see of Tours; Gregory had previously considered himself a "foster son" of St Julian, the patron saint of Brioude [*VJ* 2, 50]; and he had once been cured at the shrine of St Illidius, who had been bishop of Clermont and a contemporary of Martin [*VP* 2.2]. St Saturninus had been an early martyr at Toulouse [*GM* 47]. When Gregory explained this sudden flash, he referred to a story in Sulpicius Severus, *Dialogi* II.2.1-2, ed. C.Halm, *CSEL* 1 (1866) 181-2, and trans. A.Roberts, NPNF 2nd series, 11 (reprinted 1973) 38. Gregory also included other stories about this "mystical fire" [*GC* 37-8].

a hill and is surrounded by old buildings that are already in ruins. For some say that, while the crypt was still hidden and before its location had been revealed to any of the Christians, the inhabitants noticed a light burning in that place every [Saturday] night preceeding the Lord's festivals [on Sundays]. But no one knew what this mystery signified; men always suspected that something divine was preserved there. Then two possessed men came from the church of St Martin. These men clapped their hands and began to cry out; they said: "The most blessed Sollemnis is buried here in a hidden crypt. Uncover the tomb of the friend of God. When you have found the tomb, drape it with cloths, light a lamp, and celebrate the ceremony owed [to him]. If you do what we say, the tomb will benefit this region." As they said this, they cried loudly and attempted to dig up the ground with their fingernails. The inhabitants watched what was happening. After acquiring a hoe they dug and exposed a crypt into which they descended by a series of steps and found a huge tomb. The men who were still ill in their minds tes- tified that this was the tomb of the most blessed Sollemnis; but these men departed after soon regaining their senses. Thereafter, however, people suffering from various illnesses began to gather at this tomb; after receiving a cure they departed in good health. Among them was Litomeris, a native of Tours who suffered from an attack of quartan fever. After taking candles from his lodging he went with only one servant and approached the spot. He prayed, held the burning candles in his hand for the entire night, and celebrated vigils. At daybreak he returned to his own home; he never again endured the agony of a chill or any shivering from this illness.[25]

22. Abbot Maximus.

Maximus was a monk, a "great" man because of his name and his miracles. The book of his life, which I read [in a version] written in

---

[25] This St Sollemnis is unidentified and should not be confused with Sollemnis, bishop of Chartres at the beginning of the sixth century: see Duchesne (1894-1915) II:425, Vieillard-Troiekouroff (1976) 137-8, and Heinzelmann (1982) 696. A *Vita* of Sollemnis of Chartres, composed in the eighth or early ninth century, survives: ed. W.Levison, *MGH*, SRM 7 (1920) 311-21. In the mid-ninth century someone did confuse the two by combining *GC* 21 with this *Vita*: see Levison, o.c. 310.

verse, claims that he was a student of our Martin [of Tours].[26] Because
Maximus wished to hide himself, he decided to live in Lyon in a
monastery on the Ile-Barbe. But after he became conspicuous there, he
decided to return to his homeland. Then while he was intending to
cross the Saône river, his boat was swamped and sank, and the priest
was covered by the water. Around his neck he had a book of the
Gospels and [the utensils for the celebration of] the daily liturgy, that
is, a small paten and a chalice. But divine mercy did not allow what
was its own to perish. At the command of the Lord Maximus was
saved from this danger [and brought] to the bank, so that the Lord
neither allowed the loss of a life nor mourned for the destruction of the
liturgical utensils. That which the psalmist sang at the inspiration of
the Holy Spirit was fulfilled: "Although the just man will fall, he is
not bruised, because the Lord steadies his hand" [Psalm 37:24]. And
again: "The Lord will not ignore the soul of a just man" [cf. Proverbs
10:3].

Then Maximus came to Chinon, a village in the territory of Tours,
and founded a monastery. When Egidius besieged this village and the
people of this region were shut up there, the hostile enemy blocked up
a well that had been cut from the side of a mountain and that the besieged people used for drinking water. The aforementioned servant of
God, who with the others was shut up within the fortifications of the
village, learned of this. When he saw the people dying from devas-
tating thirst, he prayed to the Lord for an entire night that the Lord look
upon his people, scatter the wicked enemy, and not allow the people to
die from a burning thirst. Then, at the revelation of the Holy Spirit, he

---

[26] Although Gregory described several men as students of Martin of Tours
[*HF* VII.10, *GC* 45, 56], no contemporary evidence from the later fourth century
supports his claims: see Stancliffe (1983) 31, 166-7, 288-9, for the attested
contemporary students of Martin. Verse versions of saints' *Vitae* were apparently
not uncommon [cf. *GC* 108]. Gregory's friend Fortunatus had himself versified
the *Vita* of St Martin originally composed by Sulpicius Severus, and he
exchanged some correspondence with Gregory over the possibility of versifying
some of Gregory's collection of miracle stories about St Martin [*VM* 1 praef.]:
see Fortunatus, *Vita S.Martini*, prol. = *Epistula ad Gregorium* 2, ed F.Leo,
MGH, AA 4.1 (1881) 293-4, with Van Dam (1988a). In fact, Gregory had even
hinted that some poet might like to versify this book about the confessors [*GC*
praef.].

said to the people: "Let whoever has a container place [it] outside in the street and let him pray to the Lord. For today he will give you his waters bestowed in abundance, so that you and your small children will not be lacking." As Maximus said this, suddenly clouds covered the sky and a heavy rain accompanied by thunder and lightning fell from the sky upon the village. The storm was doubly beneficial to the people, since it eliminated thirst with its rain and scattered the enemy with its crashing. Everyone's containers were filled, and everyone was satisfied. After the enemy fled because of the plea of the priest, the people were saved and left the village.

Maximus died in the fulness of his days in the monastery [he had founded] in this place, and was buried there.[27] Often ill people are cured at his tomb. One young boy who was a member of the household of the cathedral at Tours fell ill. Since he was gasping as he lay down and was thought to have breathed out his spirit near the end of his life, he was brought to the church of Maximus. Immediately his fever vanished and the boy was restored to health. One of the slave girls suffered from a similar fever; when she was placed before the railings of this shrine, she was restored to health on the same day. Once information about these cures reached me, I had the boy tonsured and admitted to the monastery, and I ordered that the girl adopt a habit and be admitted to a community of nuns to serve God.[28]

23. The recluse Johannis.

The priest Johannis is buried not far from this church [of St Maximus]. Johannis was a Breton by nationality. Since he lived a life of the highest piety, the Lord deigned to work many miracles of healing

---

[27] It is not certain whether this Maximus of Chinon should be identified with another Maximus who was abbot at Ile-Barbe in the mid-fifth century: see Krusch (1885) 761 n.3. Egidius (or better, Aegidius) was a renegade Roman military commander who took advantage of the confusion caused by the arrival of the barbarian tribes to establish his own "kingdom" at Soissons with the support of some Franks [HF II.12]. Rouche (1979) 36, suggests that he attacked Chinon because the village was supporting the Visigoths. After Aegidius' death in 464, his son Syagrius ruled as "king of the Romans" until he was defeated by Clovis in c.486/7 [HF II.27].

[28] Weidemann (1982) I:342, II:291, suggests that the cathedral of Tours owned property and slaves near Chinon.

through his hands. Because of his love for God Johannis hid himself
from the sight of men. He had a tiny cell in an oratory in front of the
church in the village of Chinon. There in a little garden that he worked
with his own hands he had planted some laurel trees that now spread out
on huge wooden trunks with the pleasantness of their delightful leaves.
The holy man sat in the shade of these trees and either read or wrote
something. After his death the trees spread out their wide branches, as I
said, and shaded the area of the small garden. One of these trees
weakened with age and dried up. Then the custodian of the garden dug
out the trunk and roots, cut them up with the branches, and built a
bench on which he sometimes sat when he was weary or on which he
chopped something with his axe when the occasion demanded. When
he had used the bench this way for two years or a bit longer, he felt a
pain in his heart due, I think, to divine inspiration. He said: "Woe am
I, because I have sinned, so that on various occasions I use for cutting
this tree that such a priest planted with his own hand." After saying
this, he took a hoe, dug up the ground, cut off the legs of the bench,
put it beneath the ground, and filled the hole with dirt. [What happened
next] is extraordinary to report! When spring came, this tree trunk that,
as I said, had been buried by the man's hand was green with revived
health and put out new buds just like the other flowering trees. Today
there are shoots coming from this trunk of five, six, or more feet in
height. Every year these shoots are supported by the Lord and grow
higher.[29]

24. The nun Monegundis.

The blessed Monegundis died at Tours. She was from the territory
of Chartres. She had left her homeland as well as her parents and come
to Tours for this reason alone, to devote herself to prayer. God repeatedly deigned to reveal miracles through her. For whenever someone
developed a festering blister, the person went to Monegundis and requested her prayers; immediately Monegundis knelt to pray to the Lord.
She also gathered the leaves of a certain vegetable or fruit, smeared
them with her saliva, made the sign of the cross over the sore, and
applied the [paste of] leaves. Immediately all the poison vanished so

---

[29] Johannis the recluse lived in the middle of the sixth century: see
Vieillard-Troiekouroff (1976) 84.

completely that the ill person no longer endured anything deserving of death. Often she healed people suffering from quartan fevers or from sore throats by giving them water she had blessed. Now ill people constantly gather at her tomb and are healed. For it is not possible to list individually how many who suffered from chills, how many who [suffered] from festering blisters and were almost dead as the poison raged, and how many who were ill from dysentery were healed. But although I have recorded many of these people in the book that I wrote about the life of Monegundis, I am unable to be silent about what happened next. A maid servant of Probatus, my archdeacon, was severely struck by a quartan fever and was already ill for nearly a year with this fever. After the hands of her parents placed her beside the holy tomb [of Monegundis], she was brought back home with her health.[30]

25. Abbot Senoch.

Recently I wrote a *Vita* of abbot Senoch.[31] In that book I ended after recording many of his miracles; but since [divine] power was evident at his tomb, it was absurd for me to be silent. A boy named Nantulf was afflicted by severe blindness. He continually wept for his youth, still in the first period of life, that had been disfigured by this affliction. He sought out the tomb of this saint; kneeling, relying upon a humble prayer, he asked that the patronage of Senoch recall his lost sight for him. After continuing with this prayer for four days, Nantulf's eyes were opened and he left with his sight. Even now many people afflicted by the misfortune of chills and other illnesses are

---

[30] Gregory elaborated on the life of Monegundis in *VP* 19. Monegundis had eventually became a nun at Tours, where she was remarkably successful at healing people. She died sometime after bishop Medard of Soissons [*VP* 19.2], who had died before 561 [*GC* 93]: see James (1985) 156-7. The story about the cure of Probatus' servant might be a later addition to this chapter, since Probatus could have become archdeacon only after 591, when his predecessor Plato became bishop of Poitiers [*HF* V.49, *VM* 4.32].

[31] Gregory's *Vita* of Senoch was *VP* 15. Senoch had founded a monastery by rebuilding some ancient ruins at Saint-Senoch, near Tours [*VP* 15.1]: see Vieillard-Troiekouroff (1976) 275. Bishop Eufronius ordained him as a deacon, and Gregory also visited him. When Senoch died in 576 [*HF* V.7], Gregory was at his deathbed [*VP* 15.4].

quickly healed when they either pull off or touch the fringes of the shroud [over his tomb]. So much concerning Tours.

26. St Symeon and his pillar.

The confessor Symeon, who is said to have stood on a pillar in the region of Antioch, often offered cures to the inhabitants. After his conversion, as is read in the book of his life, he never looked at any woman with open eyes. But in his zeal for holiness after he placed himself on a higher pillar, he did not allow himself to be seen not only by an unrelated woman but even by his own mother. Even now he protects this place from the approach of women. For some say that a woman clothed herself in the garments of a man and wished to enter the church [dedicated] to his pillar. The poor woman thought to herself that in [the disguise of] her clothing she was able to do something that could be unknown to the Most High; she disregarded that [saying] of the apostle, that "God is not mocked" [Galatians 6:7]. When she came to the church and lifted her foot to cross the sacred threshold, immediately she fell backwards, toppled over, and died. This was sufficient [warning] for the people lest any other women attempt the same, since they saw that a horrible vengeance was imposed on that woman.[32]

MARSH

27. The tombs of the priests in the church of St Martialis.

Then St Martialis, who had been sent by the Roman bishops as a bishop, began to preach at Limoges. After overturning the rituals of [pagan] images and after filling the city with belief in God, he migrated from this world. At that time two priests were with him whom he had brought with him from the East to Gaul. But when they had completed their days so that they were called from this world, they were buried in adjacent sarcophagi in the same crypt as their holy bishop. One sar-

---

[32] Symeon the Stylite had earned his reputation as a holy man during the first half of the fifth century by living for decades on top of a pillar in Syria. Although Gregory referred to a *Vita* of Symeon, he may in fact have heard these stories from the eastern bishop who visited Tours in 591 and who mentioned Symeon [*HF* X.24]. Stylite saints were apparently fashionable in Gaul: see Elbern (1966). Gregory himself once visited a man who had tried to live on a pillar near Trier. The harsh winter made his life difficult enough, but bishops also resented his influence; finally the local bishop demolished the pillar and forced the man to live in a monastery [*HF* VIII.15].

cophagus was near the wall, the other was next to the first one. Since both stood above ground, it was not possible for the sarcophagus [in back] to be honored because of the sarcophagus that was in front [of it]; that is, no shroud could be unfolded there, and no lamp could be lit. The inhabitants of the region were annoyed at this. One morning when they came to the crypt, they found the tombs located on different walls. Free access to both tombs was thus now possible, and it was obvious [from this deed] how the blessed bishop was respected as a suppliant of God.[33]

28. The miracles performed at his tomb.

A girl whose one hand had stiffened (I do not know what her sin was) and whose fingers were fixed in her palm came to the tomb of Martialis. She trusted in the power of the confessor, that the intercession of the man whose preaching had freed people who were ensnared by the false rituals of superstition could also loosen her withered hand. Then, during the celebration of the vigils on the night of his festival, while she was attentively praying before his tomb, she was surprised and marveled at how her hand was healed and the fingers straightened. The people witnessed [this miracle].

A man deserved [to regain] his speech in this manner. This man, as the coarse rusticity of people behaves, swore a false oath in the cathedral. Soon his tongue stiffened and he became mute, so that he seemed to imitate not the sound of a human voice but the lowing of an animal. But he went to the tomb of this confessor and knelt in prayer. As he later claimed, he felt as if someone had touched his throat; this, as I believe, was the power of the confessor of the Lord. The man stood up and with a nod requested a priest who was present to make the sign of the cross over his clenched jaws. After the priest did this, again the man knelt in prayer. Immediately upon standing he regained the use of his voice and in his own words revealed everything that he had suffered.

[33] Martialis was also one of the seven missionaries thought to have been sent to Gaul in the middle of the third century [*HF* 1.30; cf. *GC* 4]. The church containing his tomb was outside Limoges and is to be distinguished from the cathedral in the city that Gregory mentioned in the next chapter: see Vieillard-Troiekouroff (1976) 131-4.

29. St Stremonius, bishop of Clermont.

Clermont first received the message of salvation from St Stremonius, who also had been sent by the Roman bishops with the most blessed Catianus and the others whom I have mentioned. Because of his preaching Clermont began to believe that Christ, the Son of God, was the salvation of the world and the redeemer of all. Stremonius' tomb is in the village of Issoire. Coarse rusticity, even though it knew where he was buried, never offered any cult of respect there at his tomb. But after the long circuits of [many] years Cautinus, who was given as a [future] bishop of Clermont, governed the church of this village while he was a deacon. One night while he was lying in the bed of his cell that was attached to the church, he heard the chanting of psalms, as if from voices singing quietly. Upon getting up he saw the church shining with a bright light. He was astounded and looked inside (his cell was on an upper floor across from the windows of the church). He looked, and behold, there was a crowd of people dressed in white, holding candles, and chanting psalms around the tomb of Stremonius. He watched this spectacle for a long time. Once they departed, immediately at dawn Cautinus ordered that the tomb be surrounded with a railing and covered with white shrouds. He announced that respect would be shown to that place. Thereafter prayers were offered over the tomb and the assistance of the bishop was requested. I heard this story from the mouth of bishop Cautinus.[34]

[handwritten margin note: vision in church]

[34] Stremonius was another of the seven missionaries thought to have been sent to Gaul in the middle of the third century [*HF* I.30; cf. *GC* 4]. In the seventh century his name was corrupted into Austremonius; for the later hagiography about him, see Fournier (1979).

Cautinus served as bishop of Clermont from 551, when he had succeeded Gregory's uncle Gallus, until 571; so Gregory perhaps heard this story while he was growing up in Clermont. Since most bishops and clerics had supported a priest named Cato to succeed Gallus, Cautinus' selection by king Theudebald split the clergy at Clermont into factions [*HF* IV.5-7]; Cautinus may well have then publicized this story about his discovery of the tomb of St Stremonius to promote his own episcopal authority. But Gregory was critical of bishop Cautinus and accused him of drunkiness, greed, and cowardliness in the face of the plague [*HF* IV.12-13, 31]. Gregory's criticisms may also reflect rivalries between aristocratic families at Clermont: see Wood (1983) 44. Yet as bishop Cautinus participated in the annual pilgrimage to the shrine of St Julian at

30. The man who received blessed bread from a priest.

There is great favor if the priesthood is properly respected in behavior. For if the priesthood was so beneficial to an unjust man and a persecutor of righteousness that he acquired [the gift of] prophecy, that is, to Caiaphas, who prophesied that it was necessary for one man to die for the people so that the entire nation not die [cf. John 11:50], how much more can divine majesty attribute to those who fear God and who solemnly and scrupulously respect the priesthood? As a result, according to James the appearance of a priest combined with a prayer is beneficial to ill people [cf. James 5:15]. Often simply the offering of bread crumbs that have been blessed[35] from the hand of a priest confers assistance; this fits with what I in truth learned to have happened at Clermont during my youth. A priest who was traveling by himself requested lodging at the house of a poor man in the Limagne. After receiving it, during the night he got up from his bed in accordance with the practice of priests and stood for prayer. The poor man too, whom circumstances forced to cart wood from the forest, got up very early. As is the custom of woodsmen, although it was not yet dawn he requested food from his wife, which she immediately brought. After taking this bread the man did not eat it until it had been blessed by the priest or until he had received from him bread crumbs that had been blessed. After receiving bread crumbs that had been blessed, he took them and left. It was still dark when he came to a river. He drove his oxen and wagon onto a bridge that floated on top of boats and began to cross over to the opposite bank. When he came to the middle of the river, he heard a voice that said: "Drown [him], drown [him], do not hesitate." Another voice responded to the first and said: "I would do what you suggest even without your encouragement, if a holy object did not foil my attempts. For you are aware that this man is fortified with the bread crumbs of the priest; I am unable therefore to harm

Brioude, who was a saint specially associated with Gregory's family [*HF* IV.5, 13].

[35] *Eulogiae* were bits of bread that had been blessed during the celebration of mass but then not used. They were subsequently distributed to believers, often by clerics, as tokens of friendship and hospitality: see Dalton (1927) II:527-8, and Weidemann (1982) II:224.

him." The man heard these voices but saw no one else. He knew that
these words were threats to himself. He signed himself with the cross
of the Lord and thanked God that the hostile faction could not prevail
against him. Then he proceeded to the opposite bank. With the load he
had anticipated he returned home in safety.

31. The two lovers.

Ancient tradition relates that at Clermont there were two people, a
man and a woman, who were joined in marriage but not in sexual
intercourse. Although they slept in a single bed, they were not polluted
by the other in carnal desire. Their life of chastity was a secret between
themselves. Many years later, by common agreement the man was
tonsured to become a cleric, and the woman put on the habit of a nun .
After fulfilling her days the woman happened to migrate from this
world. Then her husband prepared a tomb and displayed the body for
burial. After he buried her in the tomb, he lifted his hands to heaven
and revealed the secret that had been kept between them. He said: "I
thank you, maker of all things, because just as you deigned to entrust
her to me, so I have returned her to you, kept pure from all contami-
nation of lust." The woman smiled and said: "Be still, be still, man of
God, because it is not necessary that you confess our secret. No one
asked." Then he closed the lid and left. A short time later the man
migrated from this world and was buried [in a tomb] in his own spot.
For although they were in the same church, each tomb was next to a
different wall; one was on the south side, the other on the north side.
But at dawn the tombs were discovered to be next to each other, which
is how they remain still today. The inhabitants therefore now call them
the "Two Lovers" and venerate them with great honor.[36]

32. The priest Amabilis.

In the [territory of the] aforementioned city of Clermont Amabilis,
a man noted for his holiness, was a priest in the village of Riom. He

---

[36] When Gregory retold this story about the "Two Lovers" elsewhere, he
included some additional details [HF I.47]. The husband was named Iniuriosus
and had "senatorial" status, and he and his wife had lived while Nepotianus was
bishop at Clermont [HF I.46, GC 36]. Their tomb was probably in the church
dedicated to St Illidius [VP 2]: see Vieillard-Troiekouroff (1976) 90-3.

was distinguished for his great miracles and was said often to have controlled serpents. For when duke Victurius refused to pray at his tomb,
his horse stood rigid opposite [the tomb] and the duke could not ride on.
Although the duke beat his horse with whips and spurs, the horse stood
immobile, as if it were [made] of bronze. Finally the duke, who had
become, so to speak, similar to that horse, was advised by his servants
and dismounted for prayer. Once he had prayed in faith, he went where
he wished. I saw a possessed man who was cleansed at Amabilis'
tomb. [I also saw] a perjurer who had stiffened up like iron; once he
confessed his misdeed, he was immediately released.[37]

33. The nun Georgia.

It is said that in the same city [of Clermont] there was a girl, a nun
dedicated to God, who lived in the countryside where she was withdrawn
from the people of the city and who willingly offered the sacrifices of
praise that were suitable for God. Every day she persisted in fasts and
prayers. Then it happened that she migrated from this world and was
brought to the church of the city for burial. But when they lifted the
bier and began to carry her body on the road, a huge flock of doves came
and began to fly over her. Soaring overhead the doves followed where
she was being carried by her neighbors. Once she was brought to the
church, the entire flock was seen to rest on the roof of the building.
After she was buried, the doves flew off to heaven. It can be concluded
that this girl was properly named Georgia: she busied her mind with a
spiritual cultivation in such a way that she harvested the produce of her
virginity, the sixty-fold fruit [cf. Matthew 13:8]. She departed from
this world and was honored with a funeral in heaven.[38]

---

[37] Amabilis is otherwise unknown; his tomb was probably in a church at
Clermont, not at Riom: see Vieillard-Troiekouroff (1976) 93-4. Victurius (or
better, Victorius) had been duke in the province of First Aquitania during the
470s, having been appointed by king Euric of the Visigoths. He was a friend
and patron of bishop Sidonius of Clermont: see Stroheker (1948) 86-7, and
PLRE II:1162-4. Although Gregory admired Sidonius, he did not think highly
of Victorius, whom he criticized for his scurrilous behavior [*HF* II.20]. In c.479
Victorius fled with Apollinaris, Sidonius' son, and was killed at Rome [*GM* 44]

[38] Georgia is otherwise unknown; her body was buried in the church
dedicated to St Cassius [*HF* I.33, IV.12]: see Vieillard-Troiekouroff (1976) 95-6.

34. The broken tomb in the church of St Venerandus.

In the church of St Venerandus, which is next to [the church] of St Illidius, there was on the west end a vaulted chamber. In this chamber were many tombs sculpted from Parian marble, in which some holy men and ascetic women were buried. There is therefore no doubt that they were Christians, because the historical scenes [sculpted] on their tombs are revealed [to be] about the miracles of the Lord and his apostles. During the time when Georgius, a citizen of Velay, was count at Clermont, a section of the vaulting that was soaked with rain because of long neglect from lack of repair fell on one of the sarcophagi.[39] The lid of the sarcophagus was struck and shattered into pieces. A girl was visible, lying in the sarcophagus; all her limbs were as intact as if she had been recently taken from this world. Her face, her hands, and her remaining limbs were without blemish; her hair was very long; I believe that she had been buried in spices. The robe that covered her lifeless limbs was as [white as] a lamb and intact, neither mutilated by any decay nor discolored by any blackness. Why say more? She appeared to be so robust that she was thought to be sleeping rather than dead. Because of the shiny whiteness of her silk robe some of us thought that she had died while wearing the white robes [immediately after her baptism]. Some said that rings and gold necklaces were found on her and secretly removed, so that the bishop did not know. But no one of our present generation knew, either from gossip or from a written document, the girl's merit, origin, or name. This body lay exposed for one year, and there was no one who out of respect for mankind brought a covering for this tomb. Then it happened that the wife of the aforementioned count Georgius became seriously ill after the

---

"Georgia" is a Greek noun or name meaning "agriculture", "farming", or "cultivated land".

[39] Venerandus had been bishop of Clermont in the early fifth century [*HF* II.13]. Illidius, one of his predecessors as bishop, had been a contemporary of Martin of Tours in the later fourth century [*HF* I.45]. Gregory was particularly attached to the cult of St Illidius, since he had once been healed at his tomb [*VP* 2.2] and had dedicated an oratory at Tours with his relics [*VP* 2.3, *GC* 20]. Georgius was count at Clermont probably in the middle of the sixth century and may have been related to Gregory : see Stroheker (1948) no.176, and Selle-Hosbach (1974) 100.

death of her husband. After being gripped by this illness for a long time, she lost the sight of her eyes. Once she was freed from her fever, she summoned doctors, presented various requests, and offered rewards. But in no way could she receive a cure from them until finally the compassion of the Lord was motivated to look upon her. A person appeared to her in a vision during the night and said: "If you wish to be restored to your original sight, go as quickly as possible, find a clean stone, and quickly cover the sarcophagus of the girl who is at rest. This sarcophagus stands uncovered in the church of St Venerandus. After the sight of your eyes has been uncovered, soon you will see everything clearly." When the woman had fulfilled this command by covering the tomb with a lid, immediately her eyes were opened and she received her sight anew. There is hence no doubt that this girl who could offer such benefits to an ill woman possessed outstanding merit.

35. The other tombs of saints in the same church [of St Venerandus].

In this place are many tombs that, as I have said, have been shown to belong to believers. Next to and on the left of this tomb [of the young girl] there is another tomb that is wholly similar in length, width, height, and placement. At the top of the front side of this tomb is an inscription: "To the memory of St Galla." Another tomb is no less noteworthy for the quality of its sculptures. It has been placed on a mound between the exit from the church of St Illidius and the entrance to the church of the blessed Venerandus; some say that a monk named Alexander was buried in it. Often the dire situation of ill people obtained health from this tomb immediately after they scratched off some dust and drank it in a potion. As a result, this medicine has been sought so often that [the tomb] seems to spectators to have been perforated because of the constant profit from these benefits.

Opposite this tomb, if you walk through the door in the church of St Venerandus, you will see on the right side a small tomb placed above ground. This tomb is constructed from less elegant stone, but no one knows who lies in it. The event that I am about to relate demonstrates that there is something divine in the tomb. A beggar was accustomed to sit on top of the tomb, as I myself saw with my own eyes. But I believe that, as human weakness demonstrates, this man was involved in some improper misdeed, because with a loud explosion he was struck by the power of the man lying [in the tomb] and was tossed far away. The tomb split down the middle; still now it can be seen to be cracked. In my opinion, the buried man thought that the man who usually sat on his limbs was unworthy of himself. The blessed martyr Liminius is also buried in this church. Although the inhabitants possess the history of his [life's] struggle, no ritual of veneration is offered to him. As I said, in this church there are men of distinguished merits whose names are unknown to the inhabitants; but writings [about them] are, I believe, kept in heaven.[40]

36. The tombs of the bishops St Venerandus and St Nepotianus.

There is also the tomb of St Venerandus, the bishop from whom the church takes its name. The tomb is placed beneath a pulpit. When someone decides to put his head into a small window over the tomb and prays for what his situation requires, soon, if he has made a just petition, he obtains a result. The bishop St Nepotianus is also buried there. In this world he was a man of the highest holiness; now, with the power of the Lord he accomplishes whatever has been requested of him. Often people with chills utter their prayers over these tombs and acquire the medicine they desire.[41]

37. The monk whom an abbot watched while he prayed.

There have been great lights in the world who illumined it with their miracles just as the sun [does] with its beams. Some say that in one monastery[42] there was a monk who was diligent in praying and reading with the others according to the rules of monasteries. But secretly and in private he offered the sacrifices of prayers to the omnipotent God. For after he completed the schedule [of prayers] in the oratory he secretly slipped away from the presence of the brothers and went among the thick brambles, boxwoods, and oak trees, where he hoped that no one but God alone would see him. There he knelt in prayer. After he had knelt and prayed to the Lord for a long time, he

---

[40] Galla and Alexander are otherwise unknown. Liminius, whom Gregory linked with Antolianus [*GM* 64], was thought to have been martyred during the third century [*HF* I.32-3]; since people commonly venerated martyrs as saints during this period, it is peculiar that Liminius received no cult.

[41] Nepotianus had been the successor to Illidius as bishop of Clermont during the later fourth century [*HF* I.46].

[42] The location of this monastery is unknown: see Vieillard-Troiekouroff (1976) 427.

stood up from the ground, lifted his palms and eyes to heaven, and silently recited a series of psalms. He looked to heaven with such remorse that streams of tears gushed from his eyes. When one of the brothers carefully followed [him] and saw what he was doing, he did not keep it from the abbot. The abbot noted when the monk hurried off [again] to do this and followed at a distance; kneeling on the ground, he watched what the faithful disciple was practising. As the abbot watched from a distance, he saw a great miracle. For a flame extended from the monk's lips and gradually was stretched to a great distance and rose above him like a rope. Without interruption the flame gave off a bright light and seemed to ascend all the way to heaven. And although the flame grew and was extended into the air from his hair, it did not harm his head. The abbot was amazed by the sight but restrained himself a bit longer. At the end of his prayers the monk returned to the monastery. The abbot followed by a different road. A short time later he reproved the monk with many reprimands in order to discipline his vain glory, but he never mentioned what he had seen.

38. The fire that often appeared from the relics of saints.

I think that this fire contains a mystical sacrament, but the darkness of my senses cannot understand how as it becomes visible it produces such light but does not burn anyone. I know only this one fact, that these fires appear to just men or above just men. For a fire appeared to Moses in the thorn bush [Exodus 3:2] and to the other patriarchs in a burnt offering. A fire also burst from the top of the blessed Martin's head and entered the heights of the heavens. Often I have heard the abbot Brachio tell a story, as I wrote in the book of his life. [He said that] while he was celebrating nocturnal vigils in the church of the aforementioned bishop [Martin], relics of saints were brought by pilgrims and placed on the altar. Suddenly a ball of fire rose up from the relics and seemed to climb all the way to the rafters of the church. But, as he himself claimed, the fire did not appear to many people. The fire also appeared during the dedication of my oratory, as I related above.[43]

[43] As explanation for this "mystical fire", Gregory referred again to the story in Sulpicius Severus, *Dialogi* II.2.1-2, that he had previously cited [*GC* 20]. Gregory wrote a *Vita* of Brachio [*VP* 12], who had been an abbot in

39. Visions beneficial to my father's illness.

Nor is it absurd to believe that often the Lord deigns to reveal through reliable visions either how the saints are to be honored or how ill people might obtain medicine. For I recall what happened when I was a young boy. My father suffered from an affliction of gout and was weakened by the burning of fevers and many pains. While he lay on his bed, I saw in a vision during the night a person who spoke to me. He said: "Have you read the book of Joshua, the son of Nun?" I replied to him: "I have learned no more than the letters of the alphabet,[44] in the study of which I am now diligently engaged. I do not know whether this book even exists." The person said: "Go and break from a piece of wood a small chip that is big enough to bear this name; after writing the name in ink put the chip beneath the pillow [under] your father's head. The chip will protect him, if you do what I say." At daybreak I told my mother what I had seen; she ordered that the instructions of my vision be carried out. When I had done this, immediately my father recovered from his illness. After the cycle of another year went by my father again was seized by this affliction. A fever burned, his feet were swollen, and a severe pain twisted his nerves. As he endured these afflictions, he lay down on his bed with a loud groan. Again I saw the person in a vision, [this time] asking me whether I was now familiar with the book of Tobit. I replied that I had not read it. The person said: "[If you read it,] you would know that there was a blind man whose son had an angel as a companion while he journeyed. The son caught a fish in the river, and with his angel as guide he took out the heart and liver. He burned these beneath his father's eyes; immediately the blindness vanished and the father regained

---

monasteries near Clermont and Tours before his death in 576 [*HF* V.12]. In that *Vita* Gregory repeated this miracle but insisted that only Brachio had seen the ball of fire [*VP* 12.3].

[44] Gregory replied that he was learning *notae litterarum*. Krusch (1885) 772 n.3, and Dalton (1927) II:598, interpret *notae* as the characters of shorthand. But it is unlikely that Gregory was learning stenography; Bonnet (1890) 49, and Riché (1976) 191, suggest more plausibly that these *notae* were the letters of the alphabet. Gregory was also apparently quite young at the time of this incident, since only at the age of eight did he begin studying literature at Lyon with his great-uncle Nicetius [*VP* 8.2].

his sight [cf. Tobit 11:1-13]. Go therefore and do likewise, and your father will receive relief from his pains." I told these instructions to my mother, who immediately sent servants to the river. A fish was caught, and what had been commanded was taken from its internal organs and placed on coals. As soon as the smoky scent reached my father, immediately the swelling and the pain disappeared.

40. St Germanus of Auxerre.

The glorious confessor Germanus died in Rome.[45] Then [his body] was lifted up, brought to Auxerre sixty days later, and there committed to burial. During the reign of queen Theudechild a tribune named Nunninus from Clermont in Francia delivered taxes to the queen.[46] On his return he went to Auxerre for the purpose of devotion. He knelt before the tomb of the blessed Germanus and prayed for a long time. Then he took his sword from its sheath and, while no one was looking, struck the stone [lid] that lay on top of the venerated tomb. Although [only] a tiny fragment was struck from the tomb, the tribune stiffened up as if [made of] bronze, so that he was totally unable to control his limbs or to make a sound. Some [of his] servants who saw him lying in this

[margin handwritten: Punishing Paralysis]

[45] Germanus was bishop at Auxerre during the first half of the fifth century. In 429 he and bishop Lupus of Troyes [GC 66] visited Britain. Although most scholars have accepted that Germanus died during the mid- or late 440s, recently some have proposed a major revision by suggesting that he died during the later 430s: see Thompson (1984) 55-70, and Wood (1984). The major source of information about bishop Germanus of Auxerre is a Vita composed during the 480s by Constantius, who was probably from Lyon: ed. W.Levison, MGH, SRM 7 (1920) 247-83; ed. and trans. R.Borius, SChr.112 (1965); and trans. F.R.Hoare, The western fathers (New York, 1954) 284-320. Gregory was most likely unfamiliar with this Vita, since it explicitly stated that Germanus had died while visiting the imperial court at Ravenna. In fact, the only story Gregory knew of Germanus, that he had once helped the people of Brioude discover the correct date for the festival of St Julian [VJ 29], was one not included in this Vita.

[46] This Theudechild was probably the daughter of king Theuderic I (d.533), not the wife of king Charibert (d.567) [HF IV.26]: see Ewig (1974) 37. The nature of these taxes is unclear, although Merovingian queens and other aristocratic women controlled immense private resources that they had often acquired as dowries and from which they left legacies in their wills [cf. HF IX.26, 35]: see James (1982) 132-3. Nunninus is otherwise unknown: see Selle-Hosbach (1974) 141.

condition did not know what had happened to him. One of them approached but received no response from the tribune when he nudged him. Although the tribune was rigid, he understood that he had been censured; so he made a vow in his heart and said: "Most blessed confessor, I realize that I was presumptuous, but my piety compelled me to be bold. Therefore, if you deign to forgive me and permit me to return to my own home with your goodwill, I will deposit these relics in a church and take care to celebrate your festival every year with great piety." The holy man heard his quiet murmur, forgave him, and allowed him to leave in safety. The tribune went and placed the relics in a church [at Moissat]; every year he faithfully celebrated the festival of the saint.

Once I went with bishop Avitus [of Clermont] to the aforementioned church in which the relics were deposited. The holy bishop was observing a fast. When he entered at about the tenth hour, all of us who were with him inhaled through our noses the fragrance of lilies and roses. We did not doubt that this was shown to us because of the merit of the blessed bishop. For it was the ninth month [November]. This happened in the village of Moissat.[47]

41. Helarius, a senator from Dijon.

Helarius, a man descended from senators, lived in the town of Dijon. He had a wife and is said to have fathered sons with her. He embellished his home with such chastity and complete purity of both spirit and body that no one dared to practice adultery there. What the apostle once said when filled with the Holy Spirit was fulfilled in that house: "[Let] marriage be honorable and the marriage bed undefiled" [Hebrews 13:4]. In this place his chastity was esteemed among lords as well as among servants; then the man died. His tomb, which gleams [because] it was sculpted from Parian marble, today indicates what sort

[47] Avitus served as bishop of Clermont from 571 until 594 [*HF* IV.35]. He had once introduced Gregory to "ecclesiastical writings" [*VP* 2 praef.], and Gregory frequently visited and talked with him [*HF* X.6, *GM* 64, 66, *VJ* 48, *VM* 3.60, *VP* 2.4, 11.3, 12.3]. In 576 Avitus was responsible for the rather heavy-handed conversion of the Jews at Clermont [*HF* V.11]. Gregory used several systems of chronology, among them one in which March was considered the first month of the year: see des Graviers (1946).

of man he was and what his status was according to the ranking of this world. After he died and had been entrusted to burial in accordance with men's customs, a year later his wife became ill, died, and was washed [for burial]. The tomb was big enough to accommodate the wife too, in accordance with her husband's wishes. The top was removed. While the wife was being placed in the tomb, suddenly the husband's right hand raised itself and embraced his wife's neck. The people marveled at this and left after replacing the top. They knew what chastity the two had practiced, what fear of God [they had had], and what love there had been in this world between those who embraced each other in this way in their tomb.[48]

42. St Florida and St Paschasia.

St Florida is buried in this church. As the local inhabitants say, she had adopted a habit and was a committed nun. Not far away is another church in which St Paschasia is buried. She is said to have appeared to the men who were building the church of the martyr St Benignus that is next [to her own church]. She urged them to continue the task they had begun and to know that they were being helped by the assistance of the martyr. After she returned to her own church she never reappeared.[49]

[48] Helarius (or better, Hilarius), otherwise unknown, is usually dated to the fifth century: see Stroheker (1948) no.194, and Heinzelmann (1982) 625. Perhaps he is to be identified as the father of Johannes, an abbot at Moutiers-Saint-Jean who died in the middle of the sixth century [note to *GC* 85]: see Heinzelmann (1982) 629-30.

[49] Florida and Paschasia are otherwise unknown except in late traditions; Gregory elsewhere recorded a more detailed version of the appearance of St Paschasia [*GM* 50]. Since Dijon had the rank only of a *castrum*, a town, and not of a *civitas*, a city or administrative unit that under the Roman empire had included both an urban center and the smaller towns and villages in its rural hinterland [*HF* III.19], it did not yet have its own bishop: see James (1982) 43-72, on the disintegration and transformation of the Roman *civitas*. But the bishops of Langres, whose territorial jurisdiction (or, in an ecclesiastical sense, diocese) included Dijon, often resided and were buried in Dijon: see Gras (1955), and Wood (1979) 74-5. Benignus was an apocryphal martyr whose cult Gregorius, a great-grandfather of Gregory, had invented while he was bishop of Langres (and Dijon) during the early sixth century [*GM* 50].

43. St Tranquillus, bishop.

The blessed confessor Tranquillus is buried in this place. He has a tomb that is above ground; from it great benefit is shown to those who make requests. The people obtain medicine from the moss that grows on top [of the tomb]. I in fact received this proof [of the saint's power] there. For when my hands broke out in small blisters and I consequently suffered harsh and terrible pains, once my hands were touched by this moss the swelling went down and I immediately withdrew them in good health.[50]

44. Severinus, bishop of Bordeaux.

Bordeaux also has venerable patrons who often reveal themselves in miracles. With great faith the city honors the bishop St Severinus in a suburb outside the walls. For although I already said in the preface of this book that I would record only those events that God deigned to work after the death of his saints at their intercession,[51] nevertheless I do not think it absurd if I recall a few events from the life of those about whom I know that nothing has been written. According to the trustworthy account of the clergy at Bordeaux, St Severinus came to that city from the East. Bishop Amandus then governed the church at Bordeaux. While Severinus was traveling, the Lord appeared to Amandus in a vision during the night and said: "Arise and go to meet my servant Severinus. Honor him just as the holy Scriptures say that a friend of the Divine is to be honored. For he is a better man than you and more distinguished because of his merits." Bishop Amandus got up, took his staff in his hand, and went to meet Severinus. He knew nothing about the holy man except what the Lord had revealed [to him]. And behold, St Severinus came as if to meet him. They approached each other and addressed each other with their own names. In like manner they quickly embraced; after kissing and offering a prayer they

[50] Tranquillus is otherwise unknown.

[51] In the preface to his *VP* Gregory allowed himself the same flexibility: having first intended to write only about the miracles that happened at the tombs of martyrs and confessors, he later decided to describe their lives too. But in the existing preface to the *GC* Gregory did not mention this initial limitation. Presumably he was referring here to a statement in an original preface that he later omitted.

entered the cathedral accompanied by the loud chanting of psalms. Bishop Amandus subsequently loved and venerated Severinus to such an extent that he put him in his own office [of bishop] and considered himself to be his subordinate. A few years later the blessed Severinus died. After the burial of Severinus bishop Amandus again received his office; there is no doubt that this office was restored to him because of the obedience that he had demonstrated toward the saint of God. Because Severinus' holiness was recognized, the local inhabitants thereafter took him as their patron. They knew that whenever their city was either invaded by an illness or besieged by some enemy or disrupted by some vendetta, they would immediately be delivered from this threatening disaster as soon as the people gathered at the church of the saint, observed fasts, celebrated vigils, and piously offered prayers. After I wrote this entry I learned that the priest Fortunatus had written a *Vita* of St Severinus.[52]

45. Romanus, a priest of the same city [of Bordeaux].

In the territory [of Bordeaux] is [the tomb of] St Romanus the priest. According to the written records of his life, our Martin [of Tours] placed him in his tomb. For his tomb is next to the town of Blaye, which is situated on a bank of the Garonne River.[53] Often through the display of his power he rescues people who are about to die from being shipwrecked in this river. [When swamped] by the waves of this billowing torrent they cry out: "Have pity on us, St Romanus, confessor of God." Soon the storm is quieted, and the people reach the banks they had hoped for. It is not proper for anyone who has deserved to see Romanus' church from the middle of the river to die in a shipwreck. I myself experienced his power in a situation of great duress. A driving storm that rained for many days caused the Garonne river to

[52] Amandus had been bishop at Bordeaux in the early fifth century: see Griffe (1964-1966) II:271-4. Elsewhere Gregory included a fragmentary list of distinguished bishops in Gaul, among them Amandus [*HF* II.13], that he cited from a Paulinus who was perhaps Paulinus of Nola: see Courcelle (1964) 284-6. Fortunatus' *Vita* of Severinus still survives: ed. W.Levison, *MGH*, SRM 7 (1920) 219-24.

[53] No earlier evidence supports Gregory's claim that Martin of Tours buried Romanus [cf. *GC* 22]. The *Vitae* of Romanus that survive are very late compositions: see Vieillard-Troiekouroff (1976) 53.

flood outside its banks. As the wind whipped about the river over-flowed in huge waves. Overpowering mountains of water were tossed up that caused great fear among the onlookers. But after the blessed confessor was petitioned, by the assistance of his power he brought it about (so I believe) that he restrained the crashing and caused the channel of the river to be level. And so I entered a boat and crossed to the other bank without any danger.

46. The two priests who chanted psalms.

Two priests are buried in a village in the territory of the same city [of Bordeaux]. These were men of outstanding holiness, as this event demonstrates. For the miracle that happened during this event clearly proves that they still live after their burial. The two priests were buried in the same church but against opposite walls. The tomb of one was on the south side, the tomb of the other on the north side. Later the clerics began to chant the psalms during the celebration of the [liturgical] office. When they had divided into choirs and [each] group sang songs to the Lord, the voice of each priest joined in the public chanting of the psalms. For one choir was augmented by the assistance of the voice of one priest, while the other choir gained strength from the melody of the other's voice. This harmony was so sweet that it often delighted attentive listeners. In addition, benefits are often shown to be granted, if a faithful prayer is presented. This happened in the village of Bouliac.[54]

47. The church at Rions.

Not far away is the village of Rions. Since there was a catholic church in the village, when the Goths attacked they transferred it to the impurity of their own sect [of Arianism]. But next to the church was a large house. When it was time to celebrate Easter vigil, these [Goths], with their heretical bishops, immersed the infants in our [catholic] church, so that the people might more easily be bound to this sect after access to baptism [in the church] was denied to the [catholic] priest. But while these heretics were in our church, the priest had a shrewd idea; he prepared his ministry and began to baptize in their house, while

[54] These two priests remain unidentified: see Vieillard-Troiekouroff (1976) 59.

they were baptizing in the church. Divine vengeance struck; none of the twenty infants whom the heretics immersed in the church could remain alive to the end of Easter. When the heretics saw this and worried that their own house was becoming a church, they returned his own church to the priest. None of the infants whom the priest baptized at that time died except for the one whom God deigned to call after a proper age.[55]

48. The priests Justinus and Similinus.

St Justinus the priest is buried within the territory of Cieutat in the village of Saint-Justin-de-Pardiac. He is distinguished for his many miracles; often possessed people who are shouting are cleansed at his tomb. Similinus, who performed the duties of the same rank [of the priesthood] in the church, shares in his merits and holiness. Similinus is buried in Tarbes, a village in the territory [of Cieutat]; he flourishes with similar miracles.[56]

49. St Severus, priest.

St Severus is associated with this city [of Cieutat] and its territory. The descendant of a noble family, he was ordained a priest. He built one church in the countryside of an estate at Saint-Justin that belonged to him and another church of God in another village; he fortified both with the relics of saints. When the Lord's day [Sunday] came, he celebrated mass in one place and then journeyed to the other. The distance between the churches was about twenty miles. On every Lord's day this was his duty. It happened that on one Lord's day, while he was travelling and hurrying very quickly by kicking his horse with his heel, the branch of a medlar tree struck his head. Severus knew he had been hurt and said: "May the God at whose bidding you sprang from the ground command you to wither." Immediately the tree dried up all the way to the roots of its sap. Severus proceeded where he was going; after cele-

---

[55] Rouche (1979) 40-1, uses this story as another example of the persecution initiated against catholic Christians by the Arian Euric, king of the Visigoths from 466 to 484. But Gregory's account of the hostile religious policies of Euric [*HF* II.25] is fundamentally misleading: see Wood (1985) 255.

[56] Justinus and Similinus are otherwise unknown: see Vieillard-Troiekouroff (1976) 260-1, 292.

brating the liturgy he stayed in the same place for three days. On the fourth day he returned. When he saw the withered tree, he said: "Woe am I, who in the bitterness of my heart cursed this tree. Behold how it has dried up!" He dismounted, knelt at the roots of the tree, and said to the Lord: "Almighty God, at your bidding everything is governed and under your control the unborn are created, the created live, and the dead are renewed. By trusting in your command of salvation we believe that we live after the death of this body because of resurrection in the future. Order this tree to live again and be as it was earlier." Immediately moisture rose up from the ground as if through some arrangement of arteries and was circulated through all the branches of the outstretched tree as bountiful nourishment. The tree softened its dry knots and its leaves sprouted. The bystanders marvelled that the tree was again living. Severus had such great power and charity that, as noted above, he made his own houses into churches and he spent his own resources on feeding the poor. In one of the churches he placed his own tomb in which he was [eventually] buried. For he was accustomed to pick the blossoms of lilies when they bloomed and to attach them to the walls of his church.[57]

50. The lily by his tomb.

It is therefore apparent what sort of life Severus led in this world with the assistance of the Lord that now he is distinguished by visible signs. As time passed the lily that I said he had picked and placed in the church where his tomb was located withered; the petals of the blossoms drooped down and the stalk was dry. The lily seemed to be so dried out that if it were touched with a hand, it was thought to disintegrate immediately into dust. It remained in this brittle state for an entire year. But when the day came when the confessor migrated from his body, the lily revived with renewed freshness. As its petals revived a bit, you might see the blossoms lifted and renewed, without any

[57] This Severus is not to be confused with Sulpicius Severus, a younger contemporary of Martin of Tours [note to *GC* 4]. Severus the priest is perhaps to be dated to the late fifth and early sixth century and may have been a correspondent of bishop Ruricius of Limoges: see Mathisen (1982) 384, and Heinzelmann (1982) 693. His second church was probably at Saint-Sever-de-Rustan, where he may have been buried: see Vieillard-Troiekouroff (1976) 276.

moisture from water or from the ground, to that appearance they had previously had. In this way the blessed confessor offers new blossoms from his tomb; for with the other saints Severus flourishes in heaven like a palm tree.

51. The tombs that were raised [from the ground].

Three priests were buried in the territory of the village of Aire-sur-l'Adour. According to an ancient account they were not related by a bond of blood, but they did become allies in the love of God and brothers in heaven. Since their tombs were placed next to each other they distinguished the area of this one place with the frequency of their miracles. They lay at rest in the spots where they were buried for many years. Recently the pavement that was formed from lime and crushed bricks, [as hard] as the hardest stone, split and exposed the top of one tomb. Once this tomb was lifted a bit, the ground was split and revealed the top of another tomb. After the appearance of this second tomb a third tomb followed; after their initial appearance the second and third tombs were slowly raised above ground. Already now the first tomb is free from the weight of the ground and offers itself exposed to the sight of men; the other two tombs are still following [the first], but each year they emerge further [from the ground]. O miraculous mystery of the Divine! This mystery exposes to this world the purity of the bodies that were buried by producing them from [beneath] the pavement. It prepares for the resurrection those who must not be given to the worm or to dying, but who must be made equal to the bright light of the sun and who must be glorified by their resemblance to the body of the Lord. As I said above, these tombs are within the territory of the village of Aire-sur-l'Adour.

52. The tomb of bishop Theomastus.

Theomastus was noted for his holiness in accordance with the meaning of his name, and he is said to have been bishop of Mainz. For some unknown reason he was expelled from Mainz and went to Poitiers. There he ended his present life by remaining in a pure confession. What his reward is in heaven is revealed at his tomb; for the power coming from his tomb proves that he lives in Paradise. What the Lord Jesus Christ said to Martha in the Gospel is truly demonstrated in this man: "He who believes in me, even though he dies, lives. And everyone who lives and believes in me will not die in eternity" [John

Meylily Dust

11:25-26]. This tomb is above ground in front of the courtyard [of the church] of the blessed Hilary. Many people have scratched dust from this tomb; when the dust is swallowed, it offers such a remedy for toothaches and fevers that whoever drinks it marvels at the result. This blessing is sought so constantly that already the sarcophagus appears to have been perforated in one spot.[58]

53. The confessor Lupianus.

Within the territory of Poitiers that is contiguous to Nantes, that is, in the village of Rezé, a man named Lupianus is buried. He died [while clothed] in the white robe [of baptism]. This man is said to *Heal* have received the gift of baptism from the blessed bishop Hilary; but soon, as I said, he migrated from his body. Such favor was attributed to him by God who is the dispenser of all good that at his tomb a blind man has deserved [to receive] his sight, a paralytic his mobility, and a mute man his speech.[59]

54. Bishop Melanius of Rennes.

After the signs of innumerable miracles bishop Melanius of Rennes was distinguished in this world, [although he was] equally eager for heaven. Over his tomb Christians constructed a building that was noted for its height. But at the instigation of the evil one, who is always opposed to good works, at a certain time the building caught fire. The shroud that covered the holy tomb of the confessor was made of linen. As the flames increased, the framework of beams suddenly broke and roof tiles, bindings, and other materials on the roof collapsed. The top of one rafter caught on fire; pushed by the force of the collapse the rafter fell on the tomb of the saint. It could have not only burned the shroud but also crushed it between itself and the stone top of the tomb. A large pile of coals fell on top. The other curtains that were hanging on the walls or over doors were burned up during the first blast of flames. But this shroud was not only not burned, it was not even slightly discolored by the intense fire. When the fire was over, the

---

[58] Theomastus (or Thaumastus) was bishop at Mainz in the early fifth century: see Vieillard-Troiekouroff (1976) 224. "Thaumastos" is a Greek adjective or name meaning "wonderful" or "marvellous".

[59] Lupianus is otherwise unknown.

people came with loud cries and hurried to the tomb of the bishop. Amidst their wailing and crying they were about to receive new reasons for rejoicing. They removed the timbers and the embers from the top of the tomb, picked up the shroud over the tomb, and brushed off the coals. Everyone was amazed that it was undamaged.[60]

55. Bishop Victorius of Le Mans.

Bishop Victorius of Le Mans often distinguished himself with great miracles. For some say that once the city was being consumed by fire. As the wind blew the flames were tossed about here and there in huge balls [of fire]. Like a good shepherd Victorius did not allow the sheepfold of his church to be destroyed by the treachery of Satan. He confronted the whirlwind, and after he raised his hand and made the sign of the cross against it, immediately the entire fire died out. [The people in] the city were freed [from the fire] and thanked their pastor because he had not allowed their possessions to be devoured by the threatening fire. Often ill people are cured at his tomb.[61]

56. Abbot Martinus of Saintes.

Some say that Martinus, an abbot at Saintes, was a student of our Martin [of Tours]. He is buried in peace in a village [in the territory] of Saintes, in the monastery that he built according to the instructions of his teacher. One inhabitant of the countryside presented his hands that were contracted to the tomb of Martinus and returned with them cured. Another man had lost his mobility because his tendons had been inflamed by a fever in the fluid and his knees had been twisted. When he knelt before the holy tomb, he received new strength after the dryness was relieved and he lifted himself up with his health. Then he served there for many years . Bishop Palladius was unable [to move] Martinus' tomb with the help of many men. But when the assistance

[60] Melanius was bishop of Rennes during the first part of the sixth century: see Duchesne (1894-1915) II:344-5. A *Vita* of Melanius survives, composed during the ninth century: ed. B.Krusch, *MGH*, SRM 3 (1896) 372-6.

[61] Victorius (or Victurius) was bishop of Le Mans during the mid-fifth century: see Duchesne (1894-1915) II:336-7.

of the confessor helped, he moved the tomb with five abbots and put it where he wished.[62]

57. Bishop Bibianus of the same city [of Saintes].

Bishop Bibianus is also buried in a suburb of Saintes. A book that has already been written about his life narrates the bulk of his miracles. These days, after being entreated he repeatedly dispenses healing to those who are weak. It therefore seems best for me to undertake to mention one of these miracles. There was a woman whose hands had withered and were being lacerated by her fingernails; after the tendons contracted, her hands lost their ability for work. After she devoutly knelt before the tomb of the blessed saint and offered a prayer, the sinews of her fingers were loosened and she deserved to raise her hands that had been restored in gratitude to the Lord.[63]

58. Bishop Trojanus of this city [of Saintes].

Bishop Trojanus of Saintes was joined with Bibianus in heaven and was buried next to his tomb. This bishop is said to have had great power.[64] Once in the darkness of the night he was walking about the holy shrines that then surrounded the city, accompanied by only one subdeacon. A huge ball of light appeared to him, as if it had descended from heaven. After acknowledging the light, the man of God said to

---

[62] No earlier evidence supports Gregory's claim that Martinus was a student of Martin of Tours [cf. *GC* 22]; his tomb was apparently located in Saujon: see Vieillard-Troiekouroff (1976) 285-6. Bishop Palladius of Saintes was a contemporary of Gregory [*GM* 55, *GC* 59]. They had once met in 585 [*HF* VIII.2, 7], and in 589 Palladius acquired some relics of St Martin from Gregory [*VM* 4.8].

[63] Bibianus (or better, Vivianus) was bishop of Saintes during the middle of the fifth century. A *Vita* survives: ed. B.Krusch, *MGH*, SRM 3 (1896) 94-100. Whether this *Vita* was the book to which Gregory referred depends upon its date of composition. Although Krusch, o.c. 92, argued that the *Vita* was a Carolingian composition of the eighth or ninth century, others have dated its composition towards the middle of the sixth century and linked it to the completion of a church dedicated to St Vivianus: see Lot (1929), Courcelle (1964) 339-47, Griffe (1964-1966) II:70-71, 274-5, and Vieillard-Troiekouroff (1976) 284-5.

[64] Trojanus was bishop of Saintes in the early sixth century: see Duchesne (1894-1915) II:73.

his companion: "Do not follow any further, until I call you." The subdeacon fell to the ground and not far away watched what miracle the servant of God performed. For he was standing on public land. As the light came nearer, the bishop hurried to meet it. He bowed himself to the ground and said: "I ask, bless me, holy bishop." He who had approached [in the light] replied to him: "You bless me, Trojanus, bishop of God." After they exchanged kisses and offered a prayer, they spoke together for a long time. The subdeacon was amazed as he watched, and he saw the light that had appeared return by the same way it had come. After summoning the subdeacon to himself Trojanus said: "Come now, so that we might complete the trip we began for visiting the shrines of the saints." The subdeacon was afraid and said: "My lord, I ask that you not disdain my humility but tell me what you have seen. For I noticed that it was something divine." The bishop said to him: "I [will] tell you, but you will repeat it to no one. For know that on the day you speak openly of these events you will migrate from this world." He continued: "I saw St Martin of Tours, and he spoke with me. Take care therefore lest you dare to reveal the secrets of God to anyone." Eventually the bishop completed the course of his life and died. His subdeacon was full of days and felt badly that the power of St Trojanus was hidden. So after the bishop, the clerics, and the senior citizens were gathered, the subdeacon recounted in sequence everything that he had heard from the saint and how he had seen the mystery of the light that most clearly revealed the faith of Trojanus and the glory of Martin. He concealed none of the events and added these words: "So that you may have proof that what I say is true, when my discourse is over I will end my life." Once he said these words, his eyes were closed and, to the surprise of the bystanders, he died.

The blessed Trojanus was, as I said, a bishop of great power, and he was held in honor among all the citizens of his city. This story is told of him while he was still alive. Whenever he put on, as he was accustomed, a new cloak in which he was about to journey around his diocese, various people pulled off threads from this garment. For everyone thought that whatever he could snatch from that cloak was beneficial. Although Trojanus was buried in the ground, through his many miracles he demonstrates that he lives in heaven. Possessed men, people suffering from chills, and other ill people often pray at his tomb and leave after receiving their health.

59. The tomb in the same city [of Saintes] that was moved by divine aid.

Not far from the shrine of this confessor [Trojanus] was a small oratory. There was a huge sarcophagus in one corner where an arch had its footing. It was said that two people were buried in the sarcophagus, a husband and his wife. After these two had been clothed in white robes following their baptism they departed from this world. Antiquity claims that these two were descended from the family of St Hilary of Poitiers. This tomb was situated in such a place that not only did it hinder the passage of people as they entered, but it also made it difficult for the wall that was soaked with rainwater to be repaired, because the tomb was next to it. Therefore bishop Palladius of Saintes, who was descended from the ancient family of the wealthy Palladius, attempted with a great effort to move the tomb from that place. After more than three hundred men had joined together, he tried to drag the tomb with ropes and push it with levers. Already set in place were the stones on which the sarcophagus was to be placed. All the strength of the men who were pulling was finally applied, but they were not strong enough to shift the tomb. Everyone's face was soaked in sweat, but the overwhelming task was not completed. Cries were raised of men encouraging [each other] and shouting: "Ho, come on, pull on the rope!" But the tomb was not moved at all. Why say more? They were all worn out from the task, and at nightfall they all sought to be given some rest. The darkness of the night passed. When the new morning dawned, the bishop was worried in his thinking and asked that his men go again to the oratory. He went before everyone else. Upon entering he found the tomb standing in all firmness on the stones that he had put in place. He marveled and glorified the Lord who with his capable power accomplished what the hand of a man could not accomplish. The names of these two people have not been revealed to anyone.[65]

[65] Hilary had been bishop at Poitiers during the middle of the fourth century, and his cult had become one of the most important and influential in Merovingian Gaul [GC 2]. But nothing is known about other members of his family. Bishop Palladius was Gregory's contemporary and was noted for his promotion of various cults [GM 55, GC 56]. Members of the family of the Palladii had already distinguished themselves during the fifth century as bishops and teachers: see *PLRE* II:821.

60. St Nicetius, bishop of Lyón.

The confessor Nicetius died in Lyon. He was a man of total holiness, of great chastity in his life, and of outstanding charity. I am unable either to research or even to narrate his almsgiving and his deeds of kindness.[66] After he sent his blessed spirit to heaven, he was placed on a funeral bier and brought to the church in which he was [to be] buried. And behold! A young boy who had been afflicted with blindness for a long time was mourning with the others and followed along with the assistance of a guide. While he was walking, it happened that a voice was carried to his ear and secretly whispered: "Go to the funeral bier, and when you have crawled beneath it, you will immediately receive your vision." But the boy asked the man who was leading him who it was who had whispered these words in his ears. The man said he had seen no one who had spoken to the boy. After the voice echoed in his ears a second and a third time, the boy knew that something unusual must be done. He asked to be led to the funeral bier. He approached, slipped into the crowd of deacons clothed in white, and entered where he had been ordered. Then, when he began to invoke the name of the saint, immediately his eyes were opened and he received his sight. Thereafter the boy was diligent in serving in the church at the tomb of the saint and in lighting the lamps. But he was oppressed and harassed by some of the great men in the city, so that he could have no stipend for sustenance. Often he begged for these necessities at the blessed tomb. The saint appeared to him in a vision and said: "Go to king Guntramn and carefully tell him what you are enduring. He will offer you clothing and food, and he will deliver you from the hand of your

---

[66] Nicetius was Gregory's great-uncle; he had succeeded his own uncle Sacerdos as bishop of Lyon in 552 and died in 573. Before he became a bishop he had tutored the young Gregory [VP 8.2]; after 563 Gregory served with him as a deacon [VP 8.3, GC 61]. Gregory firmly praised Nicetius' career and denigrated his successor [HF IV.36]; he also finally did compose a Vita of Nicetius [VP 8], in which he repeated some information from his earlier accounts. In that Vita Gregory mentioned an anonymous compilation of miracle stories about St Nicetius that still survives: Vita beati Nicetii Lugdunensis episcopi, ed. B.Krusch, MGH, SRM 3 (1896) 521-4.

enemies." The boy was encouraged by this advice, went to the king, and took what he supplied.[67]

Even now many miracles are granted at the tomb of the blessed confessor under the direction of Christ. There the chains of poor people are broken, the blind receive their sight, demons are made to flee, paralytics are restored to health, and those enduring the spasms of fevers are freed. Miracles are revealed in this place so often that it is tedious to record them in sequence. But one trustworthy man told me that a few days ago four blind men had received their sight there; recently he also saw a healthy man whom he had once known to be lame.[68]

61. The tomb of bishop Helius of the same city [of Lyon].

Once I was walking to meet the aforementioned bishop [Nicetius]. While I was visiting the holy shrines of Lyon, Nicetius, who had preceded me to the crypt of the blessed Helius, invited me in for prayer. He said: "A great bishop is buried in this place." After offering a prayer I admired the tomb of the saint. While I silently thought of asking something about his merits, I noticed an inscription on the door [that mentioned] how a violator of this tomb had plundered the lifeless corpse. I was curious about the occasion [and asked] whether the events that were seen to have been depicted on the door were true. Nicetius told this story to me: "St Helius was bishop of this city during the time of the pagans. He died and was buried by believers. On the following night a pagan came, pushed back the stone that covered the sarcophagus, and attempted to rob the body of the saint that he had propped against himself. But the saint extended his arms and tightly embraced the man who was pressed against him. In this way the saint held the wretched man in his arms, as if he had been restrained by straps, until morning. The people were watching. Then the judge of the region ordered the violator of the tomb to be taken away and con-

---

[67] King Guntramn had a reputation for his charity [*HF* IX.21].

[68] This informant was probably the deacon Agiulf, who stopped at Lyon on his return from Rome, where he had witnessed the inauguration of Gregory I as bishop of Rome in 590 [*VP* 8.6, *HF* X.1]. Gregory of Tours therefore would have written at least this last sentence during the early 590s. Note though that Chadwick (1948), argues that Gregory's deacon was in Rome during the 580s and that *HF* X.1 was a later interpolation: but see Krusch (1951) XX n.3, and Buchner (1955) XXV n.1.

Moving Dead

demned by the sentence of a legal penalty. But the man was not released by the saint. The judge understood the wish of the dead man and made a guarantee about the man's life. Then the man was released and returned in safety." O holy vengeance that is combined with kindness! The saint embraced the man so as to expose him, but he did not permit the man whom he had already restored and corrected to be handed over for punishment.[69]

62. The daughter of emperor Leo.

The daughter of the Roman emperor Leo was troubled by an unclean spirit. When she was brought to the holy shrines, the evil spirit repeatedly cried out: "I will not leave this girl until the archdeacon of Lyon comes. Unless he throws me out of this vessel that I have possessed, I will in no way leave this girl." Upon hearing these words the emperor sent his men to Gaul. They found the archdeacon and as suppliants begged him to deign to go to Rome with them to see the girl. But the archdeacon refused and cried out that he was unworthy [to be the one] through whom Christ revealed miracles. He was then admonished by the advice of his bishop and went with the messengers. When he came to the emperor, he was received with honor. He heard about the illness of the girl and took himself to the church of the blessed apostle Peter. There he extended his fasting for three days, keeping vigils and praying. On the fourth day he expelled the unclean spirit from the girl's body by invoking our Lord Jesus Christ and by [using] the sign of the cross. Once the girl was healed, the emperor offered him three hundred pounds of gold. But this man was of a higher spirit and rejected fleeting riches as worthless. He said: "If you wish to enrich me with your gifts, dispense that which will benefit the entire city." He continued: "Remit to the people the tribute that is owed to your taxes as far as the third milestone around the walls of the city. This will be an advantageous benefit to the souls of both [of us]. I do not need your gold. On behalf of the good fortune of you and your family distribute the gold to the poor." The emperor did not refuse this suggestion; he distributed the gold to the poor and conceded to the city the tribute it requested. Still today tribute is not paid to the public

---

[69] Bishop Helius is otherwise unknown but perhaps served during the third century: see Duchesne (1894-1915) II:162.

treasury [from the land] around the walls of the city as far as the third milestone.

After the death of the blessed archdeacon the emperor said to his servants: "If this man loved God more than money, the church that such a minister served is properly to be honored by our gifts." Then the emperor ordered that a cover for enclosing the holy Gospels, a paten, and a chalice be made from pure gold and precious gems. Once the project was completed by marvelous craftsmanship, the emperor sent [the gifts] to the church with a trustworthy man. But the messenger who was carrying the gifts, when he came to the Alps, turned aside to the house of a goldsmith. When the goldsmith inquired of him what business he had, the messenger privately but plainly revealed his mission. The goldsmith said: "If you show agreement with my suggestion, this plan can divert much wealth to us." Through the instigation of the devil the messenger was attracted to the plan. As is a common saying among peasants, often hearts are united between the one who is greedy for gold and the one who proposes the deceptions of a fraud; immediately the messenger became the partner of the goldsmith's plan. Then that forger made similar precious objects from silver [in such a way] that they were thought to be nothing else than the purest of gold. With nails he very carefully attached the decorations that had been applied with jewels and gold threads. But he did not damage the chalice, because its jewels were solidly embedded in it. Then the messenger arrived at Lyon with his fakes. He handed over the gifts and was rewarded by the bishop. The messenger returned to his accomplice and asked to receive the gold that had been formed from the precious objects. The goldsmith said that everything was still not ready but promised to complete the task that night. At the end of dinner while they were sitting together in the room where the goldsmith did his work, suddenly the room was jolted by an earthquake and collapsed upon them. The ground split beneath their feet and swallowed them up along with their money. Alive and screaming they fell into the underworld. God swiftly took revenge for deceiving his church. Many times I have seen these precious objects in the church at Lyon.[70] Let this be

---

[70] This story seems to have been an etiological legend that explained the importance and the potency of these objects. The details and chronology were

evidence for the people, so that no one might try either to steal or to defraud the possessions of the church. For he will quickly see the judgement of God threatening himself.

63. The woman who picked up the sandals of the martyr Epipodius.

miracles at a relic-bearer's tomb

A woman is buried in a suburb next to the walls of this city [of Lyon]. She is said to have picked up the sandal belonging to the blessed martyr Epipodius that fell from his foot when he was led away to his martyrdom. Often people suffering from chills and other ill people are healed at her tomb. They drink the dust they have scratched from the tomb, and they depart with their health.[71]

64. Another woman whose husband appeared on behalf of an offering.

vision warning of a corruptive official subdeacon

Some say that in this city [of Lyon] there were two people, a man and his wife, who were distinguished members of a senatorial family. Since they had no children when they were about to die, they left the cathedral as their heir. The man died first and was buried in the church of St Mary.[72] For an entire year his wife visited this church; she diligently prayed, attended the celebrations of mass every day, and made offerings on behalf of the memory of her husband. Because she never doubted that through the mercy of the Lord her deceased husband would repose [in Paradise] on the day that she made an offering to the Lord on behalf of his soul, she always presented a pint of wine from Gaza to the sanctuary of the holy church. But the subdeacon was a sinful man and kept the wine from Gaza for his own drinking [pleasure]. Since the woman never came forward for the grace of communicating [during the celebration of the Eucharist], he instead offered very bitter vinegar in the chalice. When God was pleased to expose this fraud, the husband appeared to his wife [in a vision] and said: "Alas, alas, my most beloved wife. How did the effort of my life in this world reach [such a

---

63 particularly vague. Emperor Leo I reigned from 457 to 474, but in Constantinople, not Rome.

[71] Epipodius was thought to have been martyred during the late second century [*GM* 49].

[72] The location of this church is uncertain: see Vieillard-Troiekouroff (1976) 150. Weidemann (1982) I:340, suggests that the church may even have belonged to the couple.

point] that I now taste vinegar in my offering?" The woman replied to him: "In truth, I have not forgotten your charity and I have always offered the most fragrant wine from Gaza in the sanctuary of my God on behalf of your repose." She awoke, thought about the vision, and did not forget it. As was her custom, she got up for matins. After matins were over and mass had been celebrated, she approached the cup of salvation. When she sipped from the chalice, the vinegar was so bitter that she thought her teeth would have fallen out if she had not swallowed the drink quickly. Then she rebuked the subdeacon, and what had been done sinfully and fraudulently was corrected. But I think that this miracle did not happen without the merit of the good deed [performed by the woman].

65. Bishop Memmius of Châlons-sur-Marne.

Bishop Memmius was the special patron of Châlons-sur-Marne. While he was still alive in this mortal body he is said to have revived a dead man. I have now often seen at his tomb the broken chains and fetters of poor people; in addition, I myself personally experienced his power. Once when I was staying in that city one of my servants was seized by a fever, weakened by vomiting, and simultaneously rejected food and drink. I then suffered from a great depression because the illness of this servant posed delays for my journey. Immediately I entered the church of St Memmius. I knelt at his tomb on behalf of my servant, I wept, and I prayed that he who had often demonstrated his regard for piety and his pity by shattering the fetters of those who were burdened by their chains should supply the coolness of a cure for this man who burned with a fever. [What happened next is] extraordinary to report! That very night the ill man was visited by the power of the saint, and at daybreak he arose from his bed in good health.[73]

[73] Memmius was supposed to have been the first bishop of Châlons-sur-Marne: see Duchesne (1894-1915) III:95. The church with his tomb was at Saint-Memmie: see Vieillard-Troiekouroff (1976) 268-9, and, for his later cult, van der Straeten (1974). A *Vita* composed in the late seventh century survives: ed. W.Levison, *MGH*, SRM 5 (1910) 365-7.

66. Bishop Lupus of Troyes.

Everyone knows that bishop Lupus was buried in Troyes, a city in the Champagne. Because he was treated badly, a slave of a man named Maurus fled to the church of Lupus. His master was angry and followed on his heels. Maurus entered the church but did not kneel in prayer; instead he began to spew out curses against the saint and said: "You, Lupus, will you steal my slave? Because of you, it will not be possible for me to exact from him the revenge that is owed [to me]." He put out his hand and began to drag his slave away, and he said: "Today this Lupus does not stretch out his hand from the tomb to take you from my hands." As the wretched man uttered these words, immediately his tongue that had poured out curses against the saint was bound by divine power. The man was transformed and began to dance about the entire church, lowing like a animal and not speaking like a man. When these events were reported to his servants, they seized him and brought him to his own house. His wife presented many gifts to the church, but on the third day he ended his life in extreme pain. After his death his wife took back what she had given [to the church]. The slave however remained as a free man.[74]

67. His assistant Aventinus.

A monk named Aventinus assisted bishop Lupus. After the bishop died, captives fled to Aventinus, who presented a ransom to their master. But the master bound himself with an oath and said: "I will never accept this ransom except in my own district." He raised his right hand [and swore] that if Aventinus brought the money here, then he would immediately free the captives from the bondage of slavery. The ransom was brought there, but the master forgot his oath; while he pretended to free the captives, he was himself being bound. For immediately a fingertip of the hand that had made this oath began to throb terribly. The pain gradually increased and spread through his entire hand

[74] In 429 Lupus had visited Britain with bishop Germanus of Auxerre [*GC* 40]; by the time of his death in 478, he had served as bishop of Troyes for over fifty years: see Heinzelmann (1982) 641. A *Vita* of Lupus survives: ed. B.Krusch, *MGH*, SRM 7 (1920) 295-302. Even if composed later, this *Vita* still used older traditions: see Griffe (1964-1966) II:301-4, and especially Ewig (1978), who rehabilitates its historical reliability.

and arm. Why say more? Although the master sacrificed his arm by having it amputated at the joint of the elbow, he still exhaled his spirit. Afterwards his wife again wished to recall these captives to slavery; but she was struck with a headache and followed her husband [to death]. And so these men remained with perpetual freedom, even though without the security of any written document.

68. Bishop Marcellinus.

Embrun has bishop Marcellinus as its special patron. Christ worked many miracles through Marcellinus while he was still in his body. He is said to have made a pool for baptism, in which water is said to rise by divine power on the anniversary of the Lord's Supper. The water is brought from this pool to another that an ancient tradition instituted for baptism; but it does not overflow, [just] as I mentioned above in the case of the springs in Spain. A lamp constantly offers light at the tomb of this saint; once it is lit, it burns for many nights without any additional [oil]. Often it happens that if the lamp is blown out by the wind, it is lit again by divine power. Often ill people take the oil from this lamp as medicine.[75]

69. Bishop Marcellus of Die.

Marcellus of Die was a bishop of magnificent holiness. Once lit, a lamp usually gives light at his tomb likewise for a long time. From the oil [of this lamp] the power of the Lord offers medicine to ill people.[76]

70. The confessor Mitrias of Aix.

The famous athlete Mitrias was granted to Aix-en-Provence. According to a history of his life, while in his body he was a man of magnificent holiness. Although he was a slave by rank, he was a free

Mediocre

---

[75] Marcellinus was thought to have been bishop of Embrun in the mid- or late fourth century: see Duchesne (1894-1915) I:280-1. Gregory's account of the Spanish springs that also filled a baptismal pool on the anniversary of the Lord's Supper is in *GM* 23. For Gregory springs served as symbols of spiritual regeneration: see de Nie (1985) 93-101.

[76] Marcellus was bishop of Die from 463 until his death in 510: see Heinzelmann (1982) 645-6. A *Vita* of Marcellus survives, composed in the early ninth century but based on an earlier *Vita*: see Dolbeau (1983).

man through his righteousness. Those who read the account of his [life's] struggle say that he completed the course of [his life's] good works and departed from this world as a victor. Through his public miracles he often reveals that he lives in heaven. Once, when bishop Franco administered the church of Aix, Childeric, who was then an important man at the court of king Sigibert, seized a villa belonging to the church. Childeric said that the church of Aix improperly possessed it. More swiftly than can be said the bishop was summoned. He gathered oath-takers and stood in the presence of the king, crying out and begging that the king separate his presence from hearing this case lest he be condemned by the judgement of heaven. He added: "I know about the power of the blessed man Mitrias, because he quickly imposes his vengeance against someone who invades [his property]." Then the judges met and discussed the case. Childeric stood up, taunted the bishop, and heaped accusations on him. [He claimed] that the bishop had kept for his own unjust order the possessions that were owed to the sovereignty of the [royal] treasury, and he ordered the bishop to be dragged forcibly from the judicial hearing. Once the bishop was bound, Childeric fined him three hundred gold pieces after the judgement of those present had removed the villa [from his control]. Everyone agreed with Childeric, and no one dared to vote against his wish unless he had approved it.

After bishop Franco was sentenced and despoiled, he returned to Aix. He knelt in prayer before the tomb of St Mitrias, recited the verses of a psalm, and said: "Most glorious saint, no more lights will be lit here, no more melodies of psalms will be sung, until you first avenge your servants from their enemies and restore to the holy church the properties that have been violently taken from you." He wept as he said this. Then he threw briers with sharp thorns on top of the tomb; after he left, he shut the doors and put other briers likewise in the entrance. Immediately the man who had invaded [the church property] was struck with a fever. He lay on his bed, rejected food, refused to drink, and in his fever continually panted. Even if he occasionally became thirsty because of the burning of his fever, he drank only water and nothing else. Why say more? He spent an entire year in this illness, but his evil mind was not changed. Meanwhile all his hair and his beard fell out, and his entire head was so naked that you might think he had once been buried and then recently taken from his tomb after a funeral. After the wretched man was afflicted with these and other

similar misfortunes, he reconsidered at a late hour and said: "I have
sinned because I plundered the church of God and I brought insult upon
the holy bishop. Now, however, go as quickly as possible and, after
restoring the villa, place six hundred gold pieces on the tomb of the
saint. For I hope that after the property has been returned he might
grant a cure to a sick man." His men listened to what he said, took the
money, and did as had been commanded of them. They restored the
estate and placed the gold coins on the tomb of the servant of God. But
when they did this, immediately Childeric exhaled his spirit in the place
where he was. Because he had unjustly seized this acquisition, he
earned the loss of his soul. The bishop obtained from this enemy of
the church the revenge that he had predicted would result from the power
of the athlete of God.[77]

71. Bishop Aravatius of Maastricht.

Aravatius is said to have been bishop of Maastricht during the time
of the Huns, when they burst out for the invasion of Gaul.[78] He is said
to have been buried next to the bridge of the public road. Although
snow fell around his tomb, it never moistened the marble that had been
placed on top [of the tomb]. Even when these regions were gripped in
the cold of an excessive frost and snow covered the ground to a thick-

[77] The career and even historicity of Mitrias are uncertain: see the
anonymous edition of a later *Vita* in *Analecta Bollandiana* 8 (1889) 9-15, and
Vieillard-Troiekouroff (1976) 29-31. Franco was bishop of Aix sometime
during the reign of king Sigibert from 561 until 575: see Duchesne (1894-1915)
I:272. This Childeric is probably not to be identified with Childeric the Saxon
who served as duke under king Childebert and finally suffocated while intoxicated
[*HF* VII.3, VIII.18, X.22]: see Dalton (1927) II:562, and Selle-Hosbach (1974)
72-3, s.v.Chuldericus.

[78] Gregory elsewhere described how this Aravatius had once appealed to the
tomb of the apostle (Peter? Paul?) at Rome for assistance against the Huns in
the middle of the fifth century; the apostle replied that the Lord had decided that
the Huns were to invade Gaul and that Aravatius should prepare to die [*HF* II.5].
But Gregory's account of the invasion of the Huns was not very reliable: see
Banniard (1978). In fact, he seems to have invented this Aravatius by confusing
him with Servatius, bishop of Tongres and Maastricht in the mid-fourth century,
and then placed him in the wrong century: see Kurth (1919) I:139-59, and Griffe
(1964-1966) I:210-1, 248-53. Monulf was Servatius' successor as bishop of
Tongres and Maastricht: see Duchesne (1894-1915) III:189.

ness of three or four feet, the snow never touched his tomb. One might understand that Aravatius was a true Israelite [cf. John 1:47]. For as the Israelites [passed] between the walls of water, the water was an indication not of danger but of safety; and the snow that fell around the tomb of this just man was an occasion not of moisture but of honor. Around the tomb you might see mountains of snow heaped high, but they never touch the edge of the tomb. We do not marvel when the ground is covered with snow, but we do marvel that it did not dare to touch the spot of the blessed tomb. Many times the devotion and zeal of believers have constructed an oratory from wood planks that had been planed smooth; but immediately the planks either are snatched by the wind or collapse of their own accord. And I believe that this continued to happen until someone came along who constructed a worthy building in honor of the glorious bishop. After some time passed Monulf became bishop of Maastricht. He built, arranged, and decorated a huge church in honor of Aravatius. His body was translated into this church with great zeal and veneration, and it is now distinguished with great miracles.

72. The cemetery at Autun.

In Autun there is a cemetery that the Gallic language calls [?], because the bodies of many men have been buried there. The mystery of psalms being chanted in private is a constant indication that among these [graves] there are the tombs of certain souls that were faithful and worthy of God. As they give the thanks that they owe to omnipotent God in the proclamation of their voices, they have often appeared to many people. For I heard that while two of the inhabitants of this region were preparing to visit the holy shrines for prayer, they heard the chanting of psalms in the church of St Stephen that was next to this cemetery. They admired the sweetness of the melody and went to the door of the church, thinking that vigils were being celebrated by some monks. They entered and for a long time knelt in prayer. When they got up, they saw a chorus of people chanting psalms. They noted that although there were no lights in the church everything gleamed in its own brightness. Yet they recognized absolutely none of the people. They were stunned and struck by astonishment. Then one of the people chanting psalms came to them and said: "You have done an accursed deed when you dare to be present as we offer the secrets of our prayers to God. Therefore depart and leave your homes; otherwise you will

secret cults
take revenge

migrate from this world." One of these two men departed and left, but the other, who stayed in that place, migrated from this world after many days.[79]

73. The tomb of bishop Cassianus.

Healing Dust

In this cemetery I saw the tomb of the blessed Cassianus, a great bishop. The tomb had been scratched at by many ill people and was thought at that time to have been almost perforated. Ill people purify themselves with this dust, and immediately they feel the immensity of his power. Some say that Simplicius, bishop of Autun, is also buried there. The fierce madness of the people brought an accusation of adultery against him.[80]

74. Bishop Reticius.

Since it is a pleasure to say something about these saints, the first story must be about St Reticius because he was the first to die. His parents were most noble, and he was famous for the excellence of his learning. After passing through adolescence Reticius acquired a wife who was noted for a similar reputation of her character. He was joined with her in the embrace of a spiritual love, not in wantonness. They competed in giving alms, they celebrated vigils, and without ceasing they performed the work of God. After many years the woman lay her head on the bed and spoke her final words for the ears of her blessed husband. She said: "Most pious brother, I pray that after my death and after the passage of time you may be placed in the tomb in which I am placed. Then the partnership of a single tomb will hold those whom

[79] Celtic probably survived as a spoken language through the sixth century: see Rouche (1979) 150-1. But since "cimiterium"/"coemeterium" was a word that Christian Latin had used for centuries, it cannot be either a Celtic (or Gallic) word or the name of the cemetery that Krusch's edition seems to indicate that it was. So a lacuna should be indicated in the text: see Bonnet (1890) 25 n.1, Kurth (1919) II:119 n.3, and Fournier (1955) 451. Once the body of St Stephen the protomartyr [*GM* 33] was discovered in Palestine in 415, his relics were gradually transported to the West: see Clark (1982), and Hunt (1982) 211-20.

[80] Cassianus was the successor to Reticius [*GC* 74] and the predecessor of Egemonius [*GC* 74] as bishop of Autun. See *GC* 75, for the story of this accusation of adultery.

Chaste marriage

the love of a single chastity preserved in one marriage bed." After saying this, she wept and sent her spirit to heaven. But by the choice of the people Reticius received the episcopacy of Autun. He showed himself to be so devout that the goodness of his character equaled the grace of the episcopacy. On the day of his death he had passed through the different grades of spiritual grace in the full achievement of perfection. After his body was washed and placed on the funeral bier, the efforts of his servants could not move it. They were stunned by amazement in their minds. Then they heard from an old man [who said] that Reticius had sworn to his wife that the space of one tomb would receive them both. At the end of his statement the bier was immediately lifted and brought to the tomb. Bishop Reticius regained his spirit and addressed his wife. He said: "Sweetest of wives, recall what you had requested of me. Now receive the brother you have awaited for a long time, and unite yourself to his unstained limbs that wantonness has not defiled but that true chastity has cleansed." As he said this, the tomb was moved in a marvelous fashion, and the bones of the virgin were gathered in one place. The blessed bishop was received in the sleep of peace and was covered by the lid of this tomb. Cassianus, whom I mentioned above, succeeded Reticius as bishop. After him Egemonius took over the throne of this episcopacy.[81]

75. Bishop Simplicius.

After the death of Egemonius the blessed Simplicius was placed in charge of this church. Simplicius was descended from a noble ancestry, was very wealthy in the riches of this world, and was married to a very noble wife. Although this world concealed [the fact], their completely chaste life was known to God, even if unknown to men. Both were just and very eager for distributing alms and enduring vigils. Because of his rank in this world, as I mentioned, Simplicius was selected by the people [as bishop] after the death of Egemonius; but he was chosen

---

[81] Reticius was probably the first bishop of Autun in the early fourth century. He had a reputation as an author and opposed the Donatists of North Africa: see Griffe (1964-1966) I:102, 186-200. A poem composed at Autun shortly before 324 began by praising the chastity of a married couple and might refer to Reticius and his wife: see *de laudibus Domini*, ed. *PL* 6.45-50 = *PL* 19.379-86 = *PL* 61.1091-4, with Barnes (1981) 246.

by God because of the distinction of his chastity and his holiness.
After Simplicius accepted the rank of bishop, his blessed sister [i.e.
wife] who had previously been united to her husband not by lust but by
chastity did not allow herself to be removed from the bishop's bed.
Instead she approached the bed of her most chaste husband with as pure
a chastity as before, untroubled in the conscience of her holy mind and
knowing that she could not be aroused with the heat of a lustful fire.[82]
But the raging jealousy of a demon incites disgraceful wars against the
saints of God, and the woman whom he could not destroy by her own
impulse he tried to disgrace with deceitful words. Why say more? On
Christmas Day the citizens were aroused in a scandal and quickly rushed
to the blessed virgin. They said: "It is unbelievable that a woman
united with a man cannot be defiled, for a man joined to the limbs of a
woman cannot refrain from intercourse. For so the proverbs of
Solomon say: 'No one,' he says, 'can be pure after touching tar' [Sirach
13:1]. Nor will someone who carries fire in his breast not be burned.
We see you both lying in one bed, and can we imagine anything else
except that you are having intercourse together?" The most holy virgin
was provoked by these words and went to the bishop, who was distinguished with a similar chastity. After repeating the words that she had
heard in front of all the people she summoned a girl who held, as was
customary, a kettle filled with charcoal to ward off the winter. Stretching out her cloak, she placed burning coals in it. After holding them
for almost one hour she summoned the bishop and said: "Take the fire
that is [more] gentle than usual and that will not harm your garments,
so that these flames may demonstrate that the flames of wantonness
have been extinguished in us." The bishop took the fire, but his garment was not harmed by it. Because of this miracle the people who
were then without faith believed in God, and within seven days more
than a thousand men were reborn by the renewal of the sacred cleansing

[handwritten marginal note: ordeal / + R / miss conversi of many]

---

[82] This Simplicius was probably bishop of Autun in the mid-fourth
century; another Simplicius, perhaps a descendant of the first, was bishop of
Autun at the beginning of the fifth century: see Duchesne (1894-1915) II:174-8,
and Heinzelmann (1982) 695-6. In the sixth century men who were already
married were expected upon their ordination as deacons, priests, or bishops to
treat their wives as "sisters" and live separately [cf. *GC* 77]: see Brennan
(1985a).

[by baptism]. The church received these people and happily joined itself to the kingdom of heaven through these [new] soldiers.

76. The statue of Berecynthia.

Some say that there was a statue of Berecynthia in this city [of Autun], just as the history of the suffering of the martyr St Symphorianus relates. In accordance with the pitiful custom of pagans the people brought this statue on a wagon for the preservation of their fields and vineyards. The aforementioned bishop Simplicius was present, and not far away he watched them singing and dancing before this statue. He groaned to God because of the silliness of the people and said: "Lord, I ask you, illuminate the eyes of these people so that they may realize that this statue of Berecynthia is nothing." He made the sign of the cross against [the statue]. Immediately it crashed to the ground, and the oxen that drew the wagon on which the statue was carried were fixed to the ground and could not be moved. The huge horde was stunned, and the entire crowd cried out that the goddess was wounded. Victims were sacrificed, and although the oxen were beaten, they could not be moved. Then four hundred men from that silly mass of people gathered together and said to one another: "If there is any power of a deity in the statue, let it be raised on its own and let it order the oxen who are stuck to the ground to advance. If it cannot be moved, it is of course obvious that there is no deity in it." Then they approached and sacrificed one of their cattle. When they saw that their goddess could not be moved at all, they abandoned the error of paganism, sought out the bishop of the region, and converted to the unity of the church. They acknowledged the greatness of the true God and were consecrated by holy baptism.[83]

[83] Symphorianus was thought to have been a martyr of the mid-third century, less likely of the late second century: see Griffe (1964-1966) I:152-3, 160. In the middle of the fifth century Euphronius, a priest (and future bishop) of Autun constructed a church dedicated to St Symphorianus [*HF* II.15]; the saint's *Passio* may also have been written, or rewritten, at the same time: see Vieillard-Troiekouroff (1976) 44-5. People also celebrated the cult of St Symphorianus at Tours, where bishop Perpetuus had prescribed vigils before his festival day [*HF* X.31], and in villages near Clermont [*GM* 51, *VJ* 30]. The cult of Berecynthia that bishop Simplicius [*GC* 75] opposed in the middle of the fourth century is not readily identified: see Fontaine (1967-1969) II:720-37.

77. The bishop upon whose breast a lamb appeared.

But since in an earlier chapter I revealed how chastity is an ornament for those who love God, I recall what I heard [bishop] Felix of Nantes say when we were talking about these matters. He said that there had been a cleric in his city who had had a wife; but when this man advanced to the honor of the episcopacy, in accordance with the requirement of catholic custom he had set his bed apart. His wife received this separation with great difficulty. Although every day she argued with him that they might sleep in one bed, the bishop did not assent to such wicked behavior that the decrees of the canons did not permit. One day his wife burned with rage and said to herself: "I do not think that the fact that I have been so rebuffed from my husband's embrace happened without his own complicity. But I will go and see that he is not perhaps sleeping with any other woman for whose love he has rejected me." Immediately she went to the bishop's chamber and found him taking an afternoon nap. She approached his bed and saw a lamb of overpowering brightness lying on his breast. She was terrified with fear and quickly removed herself from the saint's bed. No longer did she continue to ask what the man who was filled with God was doing in secret. But she knew full well that what the Lord himself had deigned to promise to his believers was fulfilled with the servants of God. The Lord said: "Behold, I am with you for all days until the end of this world" [Matthew 28:20].[84]

78. Bishop Remigius of Rheims.

Remigius, I note, was bishop of Rheims. Some say that he served seventy or more years in his episcopacy and that through his prayer he brought it about that the corpse of a dead girl was revived. He often offered the grace of cures to ill people, and very often he was an avenger

---

[84] Felix became bishop of Nantes in 550 and was effective in protecting his city from pillaging Bretons [*HF* V.31]. But Gregory did not much like him. In 576 Felix had claimed that Gregory's brother Peter, a deacon at Langres, had once tried to murder his bishop [*HF* V.5], and in 580 he had supported a rival of Gregory [*HF* V.49]. When Felix was dying in 582, Gregory refused to support his designated successor [*HF* VI.15]. Gregory's use of Felix as an informant may perhaps imply that the two had somehow reconciled: see McDermott (1975a), who also suggests that the unnamed bishop was Victurius of Rennes [*HF* VIII.32, IX.39].

against invaders. Not far from the church is a field that has fertile soil; the inhabitants call these [fields] "olcae".[85] This field had been given to the holy church. One of the citizens scorned the man who had donated this field to the holy shrine and occupied it. Although this man had been repeatedly dunned by the bishop and the abbot of the region that he return what he had unjustly occupied, he disregarded the words that he heard and defended the property he had plundered with stubborn purpose. Then he had a reason to visit Rheims, although not out of piety. He hurried to the church of the saint. Again the abbot denounced him for seizing the field; but he replied with nothing worthy of rational thinking. When his business was completed, he mounted his horse and prepared to return home. But the wrong done to the bishop was an obstacle to his intention. For the man had an apoplectic stroke and fell to the ground. His tongue that had suggested that the field be taken was bound, his eyes that had coveted were closed, and his hands that had seized the field were contracted. The man was stuttering and was barely able to speak a word; he said: "Carry me to the church of the saint and throw on his tomb however much gold I have. For I have sinned by stealing his property." The man who had donated the field saw him coming with his gifts and said: "Saint of God, I ask you, do not look at his gifts that you never used to accept. I pray you, do not assist this man who under the influence of his burning lust was the wicked possessor of your properties." The saint did not delay in hearing the voice of the poor man. For although the [other] man presented gifts, upon returning home he lost his spirit and the church recovered its properties.[86]

But it is proper not to be silent about what happened when the plague of the groin ravaged the people [of the old Roman province] of

[85] The word "olca" was probably a local usage, not a Celtic word: see Bonnet (1890) 25, and Fournier (1955) 451-2.

[86] Remigius was bishop of Rheims for seventy-four years, from 458/9 until 532/3: see Heinzelmann (1982) 679. One of his most notable achievements was to preside over the baptism of Clovis: see Wood (1985). Gregory knew about his life and miracles from a *Vita* [*HF* II.31], which may be the *Vita* wrongly attributed to Fortunatus: ed. B.Krusch, *MGH*, AA 4.2 (1885) 64-7. Secular abbots, who were also sometimes clerics, were responsible for the administration of some large churches and their property [cf. *GC* 79]: see Pietri (1983a).

First Germany. When everyone was terrified at hearing of this devastation, the people of Rheims rushed to the tomb of St Remigius to request a remedy that was appropriate for the situation. After lighting candles and many lamps, they kept watch for the entire night [while singing] hymns and celestial psalms. At dawn they searched in a treatise for what was still missing from their request. By the revelation of God they discovered how, after first praying, they might fortify the defenses of the city with a still more effective defense. They took the shroud from the tomb of the blessed Remigius and arranged it in the shape of a funeral bier. With candleholders and candles burning above the crosses, they joined voices in chants and journeyed around the city as well as its villages. Nor did they omit any home that they did not include in their circuit. Why say more? Not many days later the celebrated plague approached the edges of the city. It advanced all the way to that spot where the relic of the blessed Remigius had gone, and whenever it recognized the boundary that had been set, it did not in any way dare to advance further. Because of the obstacle of his power the plague even left what it had previously invaded.[87]

79. St Ursinus, bishop of Bourges.

Bourges first received the word of salvation from St Ursinus, who was ordained bishop by disciples of the apostles and selected for Gaul. Ursinus was the first to establish and govern the church at Bourges.[88] After he migrated from this world, he was placed in a tomb in a field among the tombs of other people. For the people still did not under-

---

[87] First Germany was an old Roman province situated along the middle Rhine. It is not clear why Gregory mentioned it here, since Rheims was located in the old Roman province of Second Belgica. Throughout the later sixth century the plague appeared at intervals in western Europe: see Biraben and Le Goff (1975). In 543 the plague threatened Gaul, perhaps for the first time.

[88] By stating that Ursinus had been ordained by disciples of the apostles Gregory seems to have hinted at traditions that claimed apostolic origins for Gallic churches or that claimed a pedigree stretching back to Clement, an early bishop of Rome [cf. GM 55]: see Griffe (1955), and Gilliard (1975). But Gregory elsewhere mentioned that one of the disciples of the original seven missionaries sent to Gaul in the middle of the third century [cf. GC 4] had brought Christianity to Bourges [HF I.31]. Although Gregory seems there to have forgotten his name, this disciple was presumably Ursinus.

stand how to venerate bishops of God and how to show the respect that
was owed them. Hence it happened that as the dirt filled in, a vineyard
was planted on top and buried all memory of the first bishop of the
city. Until the time when Probianus was selected as bishop of the city,
no one spoke of Ursinus. There was a man named Agustus who was a
member of the household of Desideratus who had once been bishop [of
Bourges]. Agustus' hands and feet were so contracted that whenever he
wished to progress or go somewhere, he dragged himself in no other
way than on his knees and elbows. At the direction of God he built
from the alms of the pious an oratory in honor of the most blessed
bishop St Martin in the village of Brives. When Agustus placed relics
of Martin in the oratory, immediately his limbs were straightened and
he was cured. Then he gathered a few monks with himself, lived according to the rule of a monastery, and was always occupied in prayer.

Hence it happened that subsequently Agustus was summoned by
bishop Probianus and ordained as abbot for the church of St Symphorianus that the aforementioned bishop had built in sight of the wall of
Bourges. But Agustus did not leave the monks whom he had previously gathered; by appointing a prior for them he himself governed
both communities. While he was staying at this church, St Ursinus
appeared to him in a vision during the night and said: "Dig in the
ground and look for my body. For I am Ursinus, the first bishop of
this city." Agustus said: "Where will I go and where will I look for
your tomb, when I do not know the spot where you have been placed?"
Ursinus took his hand, led him to the spot, and said: "My body will be
beneath the roots of these vines." The abbot awoke and told this vision
to his bishop; but Probianus dismissed what the priest said and showed
no interest in the search. Then the blessed Germanus, bishop of Paris,
came and was received by bishop Probianus. After a meal in the church
house he went to sleep. In a vision Ursinus appeared to both of them,
that is, simultaneously to both bishop Germanus and abbot Agustus,
and he brought them to the spot of his tomb and begged that they take
him from that place. They awoke and went to vigils together in the
church of St Symphorianus. At the conclusion of the office of matins,
bishop Germanus told abbot Agustus what he had seen, and Agustus
acknowledged that he had had a similar vision. The next night they
went there with only one cleric who was carrying a candle, and they
came to the designated spot. As they dug deep down, they found the
tomb. Once they uncovered it and removed its lid, they saw that the

holy body was not touched by any decay, as if [it were the body] of a man asleep. They admired the body and then replaced the lid. When day came, they told bishop Probianus what they had seen. They assembled the abbots and the clergy and while psalms were being chanted raised the blessed tomb with honor. But because the levers by which the tomb was being carried were too long, when they came to the porch the levers could not be tilted at its entrance in order to approach the door of the church easily. Then the blessed Germanus raised his voice and said: "Holy bishop of God, if it is your will to enter this church, let us witness your uplifting assistance." Immediately the weight of the sarcophagus vanished and it became so light that the men dropped their levers and a few of them lifted with their hands what many had brought to that spot. So, after the celebration of mass Ursinus was buried next to the altar, while the people rejoiced. Thereafter he revealed himself in many miracles.[89]

80. The recluse Marianus.

Within this territory [of Bourges] there was a hermit named Marianus. He had no other food except the fruits of the fields. If sometimes people brought honey to him, or if he could find [something] in the woods, this was his food. Although Marianus was often visited by many people, once he could not be found by those looking for him. The men who came to search for him noticed a footprint and found a spot where he had knelt and drunk water from a river. Advancing further, they found him dead, lying beneath an apple tree. Hence it was widely circulated among the people that he had slipped from the tree and

---

[89] Desideratus was bishop of Bourges in the middle of the sixth century; his successor Probianus was bishop during the 550s and 560s: see Duchesne (1894-1915) II:28, and Mathisen (1987) 453. Probianus' initial dismissal of these claims about St Ursinus may be an indication of a rivalry with Desideratus and his family, with which Agustus (or Augustus) was associated. The precise location of the oratory that Agustus built is uncertain: see Vieillard-Troiekouroff (1976) 62-3. Germanus was bishop of Paris from the middle of the sixth century until 576 [*GC* 88]. He was a native of Autun and had been an abbot at a monastery dedicated to St Symphorianus before becoming bishop: see Fortunatus, *Vita Germani* 1, 9, ed. B.Krusch, *MGH*, AA 4.2 (1885) 11-12. So it was perhaps predictable that he would eventually visit this church dedicated to St Symphorianus, who had been a martyr at Autun [*GM* 51, *GC* 76].

exhaled his spirit; but it was not known for certain, because no one had been an eyewitness. The men who had come lifted [his body] and brought it to the village of Evaux. After washing the body and dressing it in worthy garments the people buried it in a church. Each year they celebrated the festival commemorating his death; people gathered and often were healed from their illnesses.[90]

One man from the vicinity lit a fire over branches he had placed together and, in order to make beer, prepared to brew the grain that had been soaked in water for a long time and that was swollen from the sprouting buds. One of his neighbors came and said: "O man, why are you occupied in this task? Do you not know that it is the festival of the blessed Marianus?" The man angrily replied: "O you who say this, do you think that a man who slipped from a tree while satisfying his appetite has been included in the company of angels, so that he ought to be venerated as a saint? It is better to do what is necessary at home than to honor such a saint." The other man listened and then left, and with the other people he went to the church of St Marianus; his neighbor remained at home working at his task. As a wind blew up, his house was immediately seized by the fire and completely burned down, and nothing of the man's possessions remained. Although balls of fire were lifted over others' houses that were situated nearby, the flames burned [only] this man's threshing-floor, his fences, the sheds for his pigs and animals, and whatever else belonged to him. Nothing remained for this wretched man that had not been burned by the fire. If someone thinks that this happened by chance, let him wonder that the fire harmed none of the surrounding neighborhoods. What do you do now, o coarse rusticity? Because you always murmur against God and his friends, you receive catastrophe upon yourself.

The evilness of a thief stole the oxen of another man. This man followed their tracks but then lost them on the paths of the roads that were soaked with water and in the deep mudholes. So he rushed to the tomb of St Marianus and offered a prayer. When he left the church, he saw a man travelling on the public highway who was escorting and driving before himself the oxen, along with a horse that was worn out from the journey. He had been bewildered by the road, and as if having

[90] Late traditions placed the death of Marianus in the early sixth century: see Vieillard-Troiekouroff (1976) 120.

become a madman, because of his confused mind he returned to that region that he had left. The other man recognized the oxen that he had lost and took them back; he allowed the thief to leave without making an accusation, because he realized that this had been provided for him by the power of St Marianus. For he had found what he had lost at the hour when, filled with faith, he had approached his tomb. After these events happened, the people of Bourges began to honor this confessor of God with more diligent concern.

81. The recluse Eusicius.

Eusicius was another man with power who lived in this territory [of Bourges]. Just like a hermit he had secluded himself from intimacy with men among thick brambles, and he rejected gold and the riches of this world as if they were manure. Although various people visited him because of their different illnesses, often infants whose throats were swollen were brought to him. With the gentlest of touches he felt them, and as if amused by a spiritual joke he always said: "This throat that does not permit swallowing is deservedly racked by pains." He then made the sign of the cross in the name of the Trinity and freed these sore throats from their pains and swellings. He was of such immediate benefit for people suffering from quartan fevers that he immediately restored them to health simply by offering water that he had blessed for drinking.

His [fellow] monks had two hives of bees. When a man from his vicinity was troubled by the burning of a quartan fever, he went to Eusicius, received from him the usual medicine, and was restored to health. As he wished to return home, he noticed these hives in a tree at a distance. Immediately his greed, which is described as the root of all evils [cf. I Timothy 6:10], was aroused, and he decided to steal these hives in secret. He found an accomplice [with a character] similar to himself, and at night he looked for the tree. After he climbed the tree to take the hives and hand them to his companion, behold, the old man [Eusicius] came from another direction! When he saw the old man, the man who was on the ground looked to flee but did not tell his companion what to beware of. The old man stood beneath the tree and took in turn the one beehive that the thief handed down. When he wished to steal the other also, the monk said: "Son, let this one be sufficient for now; leave the other for the man who has worked on it." The thief was terrified by this voice and jumped down. But the old man caught him, brought him to his cell, and said: "Son, why do you follow the devil as your guide? Did you not come to me yesterday and receive the blessing of the Lord? If you were pleased with the honey, you might have come to me and I would have given enough for you to have a supply, without any criticism and without your inconvenience." After admonishing him then with many other words, Eusicius gave him a honeycomb and allowed him to leave unharmed; he said: "Take care lest you repeat [this deed], because theft is payment to Satan."

On his way to Spain [king] Childebert came to this old man. When he offered him fifty gold pieces, the old man said: "Why do you offer these to me? Give them to those who might distribute them to the poor; I have no need of them. For me it is sufficient that I am worthy to pray to the Lord for my sins." And Eusicius added: "Go, you will obtain a victory and you will accomplish what you wish." Then the king donated the gold to the poor and vowed that if the Lord through his grace led him back from his expedition, he would build in that place a church in honor of God in which the body of the old man might be buried. Afterwards he fulfilled this vow.[91]

82. Bishop Maximus of Riez.

The confessor Maximus was bishop of Riez and often revealed himself to the inhabitants through many miracles.[92] Not only are the blind illuminated at his tomb, but other types of illnesses are also driven away by his miracles. I will relate an event that I recently heard about. There was a little boy, about three years old, who still sucked his mother's breasts. This boy was afflicted by a fever, and while he was being carried in his mother's hands he was so weakened that he was

[91] King Childebert led one expedition into Spain in 531 [HF III.10] and another with king Chlothar in c.541 [HF III.29]. He built this church probably at Selles-sur-Cher, where Eusicius had already founded his monastic retreat: see Vieillard-Troiekouroff (1976) 286-7.

[92] Maximus had been abbot at Lérins before serving as bishop of Riez from c.434 until c.460: see Griffe (1964-1966) II:260-2. A sermon about St Maximus has been attributed to Faustus, bishop of Riez in the later fifth century: ed. PL Suppl.3.633-40; and, as Eusebius 'Gallicanus', Homilia XXXV (34), ed. Fr.Glorie, CChrL 101 (1970) 401-12. Dynamius, a contemporary of Gregory [HF VI.7, 11, IX.11], also composed a Vita of Maximus: ed. PL 80.33-40, with Stroheker (1948) no.108.

unable to take her breast or any other food. The boy was very ill for
three days and was held in the arms of those who loved him. Then one
of the servants said: "If only this little boy might be brought to the
tomb of the blessed Maximus. Because of his merits we believe that he
can restore the boy to his original health." While the boy was being
carried on the hands of those who loved him, he gasped and exhaled his
spirit. When his parents recognized this, they wept and shouted and
threw the boy in front of the tomb of the blessed confessor Maximus.
After the doors were closed, they left the lifeless body. The night was
spent in mourning. When the next day returned and brought light to
the world, the doors of the sacred church were unlocked and they saw
that the infant boy had raised himself and was pulling himself along the
railing of the tomb as he tried to walk. For he was not yet old enough
that he could walk properly. His parents marveled at the sight and were
happy; his grieving mother joyfully took him and returned home with
him in good health. I saw the boy after he had grown up, and he told
this story to me.

83. Bishop Valerius.

The blessed confessor Valerius, the first bishop of Saint-Lizier,
revealed himself in this way. Earlier an oratory had been constructed
over his tomb, but as it decayed because of neglect the place of his
burial was forgotten. The inhabitants remembered only that he had
been buried in front of a holy altar. Bishop Theodorus then came and
built a great church by expanding the oratory in a larger space. As he
was looking for the holy body of the venerated man he found two
tombs, but he did not know which of the two belonged to the bishop.
He gathered the clergy, celebrated vigils for the entire night, and prayed
that the blessed confessor would reveal to him where he lay. He filled
two jars with wine and placed one on each tomb; he said: "It is obvious that the tomb of bishop Valerius is the one in whose [jar] the
Falernian wine is increased." At daybreak he left the church, had the
doors secured with seals, and gave his limbs to sleep. At the third hour
he got up, went to the holy church with the clergy and the people, and
opened the doors. He found that one jar had very little wine, but that
the other so overflowed from its open mouth that it spilled over the
entire monument of the blessed bishop. In this way bishop Theodorus
learned which was the tomb of bishop Valerius. But because he still
wished to know more certainly, he uncovered the monument, removed

the lid, and found the venerable body completely intact. No hair had
fallen from it, the beard was not spotted, and no deterioration or decay
was seen on the skin. Everything was untouched, as if it had been
recently buried, and such a sweet fragrance reeked from the tomb that
there was no doubt that a friend of God was buried there. Valerius had a
cushion of laurel leaves beneath him; bishop Theodorus took some
leaves and offered them as medicine to many ill people. He also took
relics from his garments. After the tomb was again closed, he honored
the venerable bishop. In the future he recognized many miracles
[performed] by these relics.[93]

84. Bishop Silvester of Chalon-sur-Saône.

The most blessed Silvester governed the church at Chalon-sur-
Saône. After serving in the episcopacy for forty-two years, he was full
of days and powers and he migrated to the Lord.[94] He had a bed that was
woven from slender ropes. When ill people who were tormented by
quartan fevers or by different fevers were placed beneath this bed once
and then a second time, immediately they were cured by the power
granted by God. As a result this bed was moved into the sanctuary of
the cathedral, where it glowed with the same power. As I saw with my
own eyes, many people cut off tiny pieces of that rope and carried them
far away; when these pieces are placed on ill people, the people observe
that the blessing of health is present. My mother cut a small piece
from this rope and hung it from the neck of a girl who was feverish
with chills; immediately the illness was checked and my mother saw
that the girl was healthy.

[93] Valerius is otherwise unknown; Theodorus was bishop in the mid-sixth
century: see Duchesne (1894-1915) II:99, and Vieillard-Troiekouroff (1976) 261-
2.

[94] Silvester had been bishop of Chalon-sur-Saône during the late fifth and
early sixth centuries: see Duchesne (1894-1915) II:193. Although Silvester's
bed was moved into the cathedral at Chalon-sur-Saône that bishop Agricola
constructed [*HF* V.45, *GC* 85], his body was buried in a church dedicated to St
Marcellus at Saint-Marcel-lès-Chalon [*GM* 52]: see Vieillard-Troiekouroff (1976)
264-5.

85. The recluse Desideratus in the same territory.

Desideratus was a priest at this city [of Chalon-sur-Saône]. I saw him in the monastery at Gourdon. He was a man distinguished for his holiness, and with his prayers he often put an end to the chills of people suffering from toothaches and other illnesses. He was not a total recluse; that is, although he did not leave his cell, whoever wished saw him in his cell. As I said, he was noted for his outstanding miracles and was conspicuous in this world. When the blessed bishop Agricola [of Chalon-sur-Saône] heard of his death, he sent his archdeacon to bring the blessed man to a cemetery in the city; but because the monks resisted, the archdeacon did not accomplish what he had been ordered. Later the bishop built a hospital for lepers in a suburb [of the city], and having gathered the abbots and the entire clergy in its church, he transferred the blessed body and with great respect buried it in the church mentioned above.[95] Desideratus reveals through his great miracles that he now lives with Christ.[96]

[95] Desideratus died during the episcopacy of Agricola, who served as bishop of Chalon-sur-Saône from 532 until 580 [*HF* V.45]. In 549 Agricola attended a council at Orléans. Canon 15 of that council praised the hospital that king Childebert had founded at Lyon, and canon 21 urged bishops to care for the lepers in their own communities: ed. C.de Clercq, *CChrL* 148A (1963) 153, 156. This hospital at Chalon-sur-Saône was perhaps Agricola's response to this council's recommendation.

[96] At this point one ninth-century manuscript inserted a chapter about Johannes, an abbot who died in the middle of the sixth century. "Abbot Johannes lived in the district of Tonnerre, in the diocese of Langres. He was a man noted for his holiness and, in accordance with the etymology of his name, heralded by divine grace. When he wished to build the monastery called Moutiers-Saint-Jean, it is said that the brothers greatly suffered from a lack of water. Johannes found a deep well of great size in which a poisonous serpentine cobra lived. Once he invoked the Lord, the serpent was killed and the well cleansed. When the well [water] was fit for drinking, Johannes gave it to the brothers. As I was travelling to Lyon [or perhaps to Laon], I was graciously received by the brothers of the monastery and drank some of this water because of its miraculous power; for many people suffering from chills are cured by drinking this water. This [following] miracle is also told about the aforementioned man [Johannes]. A man who had murdered his brother was bound in iron chains because of the enormity of his crime. He was ordered to make a pilgrimage and visit the shrines of the saints for seven years. When he had arrived at Rome, he learned from a divine revelation that he could not be

86. Abbot Sequanus.

Sequanus, an abbot in the territory of Langres, was a man of great power. While alive he often freed men from the bond of diabolical obligation; after his death, through his own merits at his tomb he allowed men who were bound by the chain of a prison to depart as free men. King Guntramn lost a horn that had been taken in theft. With the sound of this horn he had been accustomed to collect his Molossian hounds or to scatter herds of antlered [deer] in the forest. This theft [made him] throw many men into chains and deprive some men of their possessions. Three of these men sought the shrine of the afore-mentioned confessor. When king Guntramn learned of this, he ordered the men to be bound in chains and fetters. This was done. In the middle of the night a light that was brighter than a human light appeared in the church. The bolts of the iron fetters on their feet broke, the links of the chains were shattered, and the captives were released. The king was terrified when he heard of this, and he quickly endowed them with the power of a free choice.[97]

87. Bishop Marcellus of Paris.

Bishop Marcellus of Paris once expelled a huge serpent from his city, as is read in his *Vita*. He is now buried in a village [in the terri-tory] of this city. The priest Ragnimodus, who is now bishop of Paris,

---

forgiven until he had journeyed to the relics of the holy body of Johannes, abbot of Moutiers-Saint-Jean. He visited shrines here and there and finally came to the church where the most holy body of Johannes was placed [not] far from his monastery. After he lay there, praying and keeping vigils, he was freed from all his bonds. Johannes was a just and religious man, and like Moses the lawgiver he lived for one hundred and twenty years. His eyes never dimmed and his teeth never fell out. He was a teacher of that notable man [Sequanus], concerning whom I will speak below [in *GC* 86]." Krusch (1885) 803, argued that the chapter was an interpolation derived from later accounts. A *Vita* of Johannes survives, composed by Jonas during the seventh century: ed. B.Krusch, *MGH*, SRM 3 (1896) 505-17, with Wood (1981). According to this *Vita*, Johannes' father was Hilarius, who might be Hilarius of Dijon [*GC* 41]: see Heinzelmann (1982) 629-30, and Vieillard-Troiekouroff (1976) 178-9.

[97] King Guntramn reigned from 561 until 592; Sequanus died sometime before or during his reign. His monastery and this church were located at Saint-Seine-l'Abbaye: see Vieillard-Troiekouroff (1976) 274-5.

went to Marcellus' tomb with a quartan fever. He knelt and for an entire day was occupied in fasting and praying; when evening came, he slept. A short while later he awoke from his sleep and rose from the tomb as a healthy man.[98]

88. Bishop Germanus of the same city [of Paris].

King Chilperic visited Paris. On the day after the king entered the city a paralyzed man who was sitting in the colonnade of the church of St Vincentius, in which the body of the blessed Germanus is buried, was cured. At daybreak, while the people watched, he gave thanks to the blessed bishop [Germanus]. For often the mobility of paralyzed people and the sight of the blind are restored by the power of the saint there [at his tomb]. Rarely is there one of his festivals during which his power is not revealed there.[99]

[98] If a truly historical figure, Marcellus may have served as bishop of Paris at the end of the fourth century: see Griffe (1964-1966) I:305. Gregory probably learned of this story about Marcellus and the dragon from Fortunatus, *Vita Marcelli* 40-8, ed. B.Krusch, *MGH*, AA 4.2 (1885) 53-4. Since Fortunatus had dedicated this *Vita* to bishop Germanus of Paris, he had completed it by 576, when Ragnimodus succeeded Germanus as bishop [*GC* 88]. For later folklore about Marcellus and the dragon, see Le Goff (1980a).

[99] Germanus was bishop of Paris from the middle of the sixth century until his death in 576 [*HF* V.8]. Since he visited Tours for a festival of St Martin in 574 [*VM* 2.12], Gregory had probably met him. During his lifetime Germanus distinguished himself by confronting Frankish kings [*HF* IV.26, 51] and by assisting in the discovery of the tomb of St Ursinus at Bourges [*GC* 79]; as a saint after his death he saved prisoners from a fire [*HF* VIII.33]. For his other miracles, Gregory referred readers [*HF* V.8] to a *Vita* by Fortunatus: ed. B.Krusch, *MGH*, AA 4.2 (1885) 11-27, and again in *MGH*, SRM 7 (1920) 372-418. King Chilperic reigned from 561 until 584 [*HF* VI.46]. Germanus was buried in a church dedicated to St Vincentius of Saragossa [*GM* 89] that king Childebert had built after bringing back relics of the saint from an expedition into Spain [*HF* III.29, IV.20]. In consequence, the church later was named after St Germanus as Saint-Germain des Prés: see Vieillard-Troiekouroff (1976) 211-14.

89. The nun Genovefa.

St Genovefa is also buried there in the church of the holy apostles.[100] While alive in her body she was so distinguished for her power that she raised a dead man. Petitions delivered at her tomb often receive a favorable decision. The fevers of people suffering from chills very often are extinguished by her power.

90. The tomb of the blessed Lusor.

The blessed Lusor is buried in Déols, a village in the territory of Bourges. He was the son of Leucadius, [who was] once a senator, and he is said to migrated from this world [while dressed] in the white robe [of someone recently baptized]. His tomb was placed in a crypt on top of the pavement and had wonderful sculptures [made] from Parian marble. It happened that once St Germanus, bishop of Paris, was celebrating vigils at this tomb. He had at hand a bench on which he bent his knees when necessary. Then it happened that during one night of the vigils, while they were chanting the psalms from the text of David, some clerics were fatigued from the effort of standing. By bending the joints of their elbows they propped themselves on the tomb of the saint, as if for some alleviation. Instantly the tomb of the blessed confessor shook, and by its immediate vibration it indicated that an insult was being committed against itself. Bishop Germanus was terrified with fear and ordered the dozing men to be removed from the top [of the tomb]. He said: "O lazy men, stand back from the tomb lest the saint of God be annoyed." Once the men were removed, they no longer felt this vibration.

It is not proper to pass over this event. The same blessed Lusor appeared to a poor man in a vision and ordered him to cleanse the small

---

[100] Genovefa (now Geneviève) lived near Paris during the mid- and later fifth century. A *Vita* still survives: ed. B.Krusch, *MGH*, SRM 3 (1896) 215-38. Although Krusch dated the composition of this *Vita* to the later eighth century, Kurth (1919) II:1-96, properly reassigned it to the early sixth century; Heinzelmann and Poulin (1986), now provide a superb commentary on the life and *Vita* of Genovefa. The church in which she was buried was built by king Clovis and his queen Clotild, who were also buried in it [*HF* II.43, IV.1]. Although Gregory referred to it as both the church of the holy apostles and the church of St Peter, it may also have been originally dedicated to St Genovefa: see Vieillard-Troiekouroff (1976) 206-8.

room in which, some say, an infant had burst out crying. After being warned a second time the poor man still put off doing what he had been warned. Lusor appeared to him a third time and said: "If you do what I command, you will receive one small gold piece for the service of your obedience." Then the poor man got up and swept the room with a broom. After washing it with water and sprinkling it with herbs, he stood in anticipation, not seeing the recompense that had been promised until by the will of God he saw the gold coin gleaming on the pavement. He picked it up and left in happiness.[101]

91. Bishop Maximinus of Trier.

[Buried] in a suburb of Trier, St Maximinus is an effective advocate with God on behalf of the people of the city. Glorious miracles are often witnessed at his tomb. During the reign of king Theudebert a priest named Arboast disputed with a Frank in the presence of the king. While the argument went on, the king visited the city's shrines for prayer. The shrines were in the villages of Trier. When the king saw that the priest's accusation was cunning, he turned to him and said: "If your accusations are true, confirm them with an oath on the tomb of bishop Maximus!" The priest said: "I dare to fulfill this command that you order." Immediately he placed his hand on the holy tomb and said: "May I be struck down by the power of the saint if I say anything false about those affairs that my accusation has alleged against this Frank." The barbarian complained and was almost angry with the saint of God. Then they left the church. As they were walking together on the road, suddenly the priest stumbled, fell to the ground, and died. Then the

[101] Lusor is otherwise unknown. His father Leucadius (or Leocadius) was thought to have welcomed Christianity to Bourges in the later third century and to have turned his house into a church [*HF* I.31]. The crypt and the small room may perhaps both be identified with an oratory beneath a church: see Vieillard-Troiekouroff (1976) 108-9, who also includes photographs of the sarcophagi of Leocadius and Lusor that still survive. Leocadius was said to have been a member of the family of Vectius Epagatus (or Vettius Epagathus), who had been a martyr at Lyon in 177 [*GM* 48]. Gregory's paternal grandmother was named Leucadia (or Leocadia) and also claimed descent from Vettius Epagathus [*VP* 6.1]; so his remarks about Lusor and Leocadius were perhaps derived from family traditions. Bishop Germanus of Paris perhaps visited Lusor's tomb at Déols when he visited Bourges [*GC* 79].

barbarian praised the power of St Maximinus, whom he had previously
criticized.

Likewise the archdeacon of Trier, after he was attacked with an
accusation of adultery by bishop Nicetius, sought to clear himself with
an oath at the tomb of St Maximinus. He first entered the door of the
crypt and stood still like a stunned man; then he went down the steps
and came to another door. But when he wished to approach the third
door, immediately he was struck with a fever and did not dare to walk
any further. Placed in danger of dying, he confessed the crime of which
he was accused and begged the people that they request assistance for
him either from the holy bishop [St Maximinus] or from their own
bishop [Nicetius]. But as soon as he confessed he was immediately
rescued from the attack of the fever and restored to the love of his
bishop.[102]

92. Bishop Nicetius of the same city [of Trier].

Nicetius was bishop of this city, as I said above. While he lived in
his body he was distinguished by the merit of his almsgiving, his love,
and his complete holiness. After he migrated from this world he was
buried in the church of St Maximinus, his predecessor [as bishop].
Now the chains of men in bonds are broken at his tomb, people suffering from the possession of an attack by demons are freed after the
demons have been expelled, and the eyes of the blind are often flooded
with light after the darkness has been removed. What will I say about
perjuries? If anyone dared to swear a false oath there, immediately he
was corrected by divine retribution. Nor does anyone dare to say either

[102] Maximinus was bishop at Trier during the first half of the fourth
century [*HF* I.37]. After bishop Athanasius of Alexandria stayed in Trier during
various exiles, bishop Maximinus became a firm supporter of both him and his
theology: see Griffe (1964-1966) I:203-11. A *Vita* of Maximinus survives,
composed during the ninth century but perhaps based on an eighth-century
version: ed. B.Krusch, *MGH*, SRM 3 (1896) 74-82. During the sixth century
oaths became a common means for both Romans and barbarians to clear
themselves of accusations: see James (1983), and Wood (1986) 14-18, for
discussion and further references.

these things or that he intends to resolve a suit there, if because of his tormented conscience he knows that he is guilty.[103]

93. Bishop Medard of Soissons.

The glorious confessor Medard is buried in Soissons. I have seen the fetters of wretched men often broken at his tomb. After a book about his miracles was written, a woman with crippled hands piously sought the assistance of the blessed bishop. With the other people she celebrated vigils with a pure faith. She was confident that her hands that were afflicted with swelling could be cured by the power of Medard who had released the chains of wretched men by the might of his power. It happened that while mass was being celebrated the withered bands of her nerves were loosened; she gave thanks to the confessor, approached the holy altar, and in good health received the grace of a blessing.[104]

Before the church was built there was over the tomb of St Medard a chapel constructed from small branches. Because this chapel was removed after the dedication of the church, it is proper that I record a great event regarding a small piece of wood [from these branches]. For often the pointed toothpicks that were quickly made from this wood have brought relief to toothaches. Charimeris, who is now the referendary of king Childebert,[105] was suffering from a toothache. When he heard

---

[103] On the basis of information from his friend Aredius, whom Nicetius had taught and ordained [*HF* X.29, *GC* 9], Gregory composed a *Vita* of Nicetius [*VP* 17 praef.]. Nicetius was bishop of Trier from 525/526 until his death in the later 560s. During his episcopacy he feuded with several Frankish kings; with the assistance of St Maximinus he also once saved Trier from the plague [*VP* 17.4]: see Gauthier (1980) 172-89.

[104] Medard was bishop of Soissons for fifteen years in the middle of the sixth century: see Heinzelmann (1982) 651. After his death, both king Chlothar (who died in 561) and his son Sigibert promoted Medard's cult by constructing a church in his honor at Soissons [*HF* IV.19]; eventually they were themselves both buried in it [*HF* IV.21, 51]. Since Gregory owned the saint's staff, perhaps he had also placed relics of St Medard in the church in a village near Tours [*VP* 19.2]: see Vieillard-Troiekouroff (1976) 119-20. A *Vita* of Medard survives: ed. B.Krusch, *MGH*, AA 4.2 (1885) 67-73; although wrongly attributed to Fortunatus, it was composed before the death of king Theudebert II in 612.

[105] Although it was common for *referendarii* (royal secretaries) eventually to become bishops, Gregory preferred that lesser clerics be promoted as bishops

[handwritten marginal note: No More pretty than death raising, all poser of god.]

about these toothpicks, he went to the church of St Medard to obtain [a piece of] the wood, so that he might deserve to receive medicine from the power of the saint. Upon his arrival he found the door closed. Because he was confident that the power of the blessed man was present everywhere, he took out his knife and cut off a sliver of wood from the door. As soon as it touched his teeth the aching pain vanished. I myself have the staff of Medard, from which ill people have often found medicine.

94. Bishop Albinus of Angers.

Recently the priest Fortunatus wrote a book about the life of the confessor Albinus, who through the gift of his merit demonstrates that miracles are revealed at his tomb. The day of his festival had come. A paralyzed man who was lame in all his limbs was carried on a wagon and sat before the glass [windows] in the apse where the holy limbs were buried. He fell asleep and saw a man who came to him and said to him: "How long do you sleep? Do you not wish to be cured?" The paralyzed man said: "If only I might deserve to be cured!" The man said to him: "When you hear the bell sounding for prayers at the third hour, immediately rise and enter the church to which you have come. For at that hour it will happen that the blessed Martin will enter the church with his companion Albinus so that after offering a prayer he should go to his festival at Tours. If you are present at that moment, you will be cured." The man did not hesitate and approached the tomb of St Albinus when the bell sounded. As the clerics began to chant the *Laudatio* of a psalm by David, a sweet fragrance filled the church of St Albinus. After his feet were straightened, the man stood up with his health. The region nourished [by the saint] testifies that many people, not just a few, witnessed this. So also a woman from the village of Crû who was blind from birth invoked the name of St Albinus and received her sight on that day [of his festival].[106]

[*HF* VI.46]. In 588 Charimeris became bishop of Verdun [*HF* IX.23]: see Selle-Hosbach (1974) 34-5, 68.

[106] Albinus served as bishop of Angers for about twenty years before his death in c.550. His body was buried in this church at Angers only until the later 550s, when bishop Eutropius, his successor, moved it to the church of St Germanus at Auxerre [*GC* 40]: see Fortunatus, *Vita Albini* 54-6, ed. B.Krusch,

95. The confessor Hospitius.

Hospitius was a great servant of God in the region of Nice. After being distinguished by many miracles he migrated from this world.[107] While he was being buried, a man put his hand on the tomb and scratched up a bit of dust that he wrapped in a rough linen cloth and carried with him. As he intended to set out the next day he found in port a ship that was prepared to go to Marseilles; but this man wished to visit the monastery of Lérins. The men who owned the ship were descended from the race of Jews. For this reason the man did not wish to indicate to the ship-owners what he was carrying. After they had advanced and come near the monastery at Lérins, the ship stopped in the middle of the sea and did not move in any direction, even though the winds were blowing. Since the Jews were confounded at what this was, the man revealed the truth and said: "I have with me relics of the blessed Hospitius, and now I wish to visit Lérins. I was afraid to tell you this. Now however I know that your ship is being held by his power. It cannot move forwards from here until you agree [to go] there where I intended to go." Once the Jews heard this, they were aroused from their amazement and changed the sails. After they left the man on the island of Lérins, a favorable wind blew and they departed without hindrance to wherever they wished.

MGH, AA 4.2 (1885) 32, with Vieillard-Troiekouroff (1976) 34-5. Fortunatus had dedicated this *Vita* to bishop Domitianus of Angers, who had died by 572: see Krusch (1885) 808 n.4. Although he had therefore written the *Vita* years before Gregory seems to have written, or rewritten, most of his *GC* in the later 580s, Gregory still claimed that Fortunatus had "recently" composed this *Vita*; so perhaps Gregory here included in his *GC* some notes he had made earlier, but without adequately revising them.

[107] The ascetic Hospitius (or Hospicius) died in 581. Elsewhere Gregory described his life and the miracles he performed while alive [*HF* VI.6]. Hospitius dressed in a hair shirt, wrapped chains around his body, ate only bread, dates, and roots, and lived in a tower near Nice; Lombards invading the region [cf. *HF* IV.44] understandably mistook him for an imprisoned murderer. After the saint healed one deaf and mute man, a companion announced that Hospitius was comparable to the famous saints of Rome. Upon his death, the worms that had previously infested his body left. Gregory heard these stories from this formerly deaf and mute man; he also mentioned that he had heard about a *Vita* of Hospitius composed by many writers.

96. The hermit whose pot was made of wood.

Behold what kind of wealth, and behold how much of the wealth of this world poverty gathers for his [saints], so that not only does the Redeemer who created everything from nothing give them what they wish, but he also orders the very elements [of nature] to be obedient to them. For I recall a story I heard years ago. In the wilderness of some region there was a man who received with the full love of his soul the brother who came from the neighborhood in ready devotion to look for him. Then they entered a tiny cottage, offered a prayer, and sat down. After they talked at length about the word of God, the old man arose from his seat, entered his garden, and collected some vegetables as food. After lighting the fireplace he put a wooden pot over the fire, filled it with water and the vegetables, and stoked the fire. He made the pot so boiling hot that it was thought to be made of bronze. The man who was visiting watched this, until aroused from his amazement he asked what this was. The old man replied: "I have already lived in this wilderness for many years, but at the command of God I have always prepared food for refreshing my frail body in this pot." When the food was cooked, they sang the hymns that were owed to God and both were refreshed by the service of this pot. This is the story I once heard. Recently I met an abbot who named the old man as Ingenuus and claimed that he himself lived within the territory of Autun and that often he had shared with the old man either a vegetable or a herb that had been cooked in this pot. He insisted with an oath that he had seen this pot become very hot after it was placed over the flames and that the bottom of the pot always remained so moist that it was thought to be continually dampened by someone.

97. The confessor Avitus of Orléans.

Avitus was an abbot in a district of Chartres that people call Le Perche. Through the revelation of the Holy Spirit he often predicted the destruction of his body. When he departed from his body, he was buried with honor in Orléans. The faithful Christians built a church over his tomb. After his death the day commemorating the anniversary of his ascension was venerated with great honor. When the others went to the solemn celebration of mass one of the citizens took a hoe and went to trench his vineyard. Although many complained about why he was absent from this festival, he refused to return and said: "The man whom you venerate was also a working man." But when he entered the vineyard and opened the ground with his first blow, immediately his neck was twisted and his face was turned around to the back. The people were watching. Then he was afraid, and weeping loudly he went to the church of St Avitus. A few days later, after he prayed continuously in the same place, his neck was straightened and he was well.[108]

98. Abbot Cyprian of Périgueux.

Abbot Cyprian of Périgueux was a man of magnificent holiness through whom God deigned to work many miracles in this world. He frequently healed people who were lame in their hands, restored mobility to paralyzed people and sight to the blind, and reinstated to their previous health three lepers who had been anointed with oil. Now also he repeatedly dispenses cures to ill people if they faithfully seek and pray at his tomb.[109]

99. Abbot Eparchius of Angoulême.

Ill people are also often healed at the tomb of Eparchius, a hermit at Angoulême. For both the fevers of people suffering from chills and other misfortunes are extinguished by his merits. When a blind man from the territory of Périgueux threw himself before the tomb and offered a prayer, he deserved to receive his sight. A count of the aforementioned city of Angoulême ordered that a thief who had been apprehended and handed over for punishment be condemned to the gallows. As the thief was being led to his death, he began to invoke the name of St Eparchius; after being brought to the post, he offered a prayer [while] on the ground and then was hung up on the gallows and left. Because

---

[108] In 523 abbot Avitus had warned king Chlodomer against killing the Burgundian king Sigismund, whom he had captured [*HF* III.6, V.18, *GM* 74]. Gregory had probably visited this church of St Avitus, since in 585 king Guntramn had visited him at Orléans in his lodgings near the church [*HF* VIII.2]: see Vieillard-Troiekouroff (1976) 175-6, 200, 247. A *Vita* of Avitus survives: ed. B.Krusch, *MGH*, SRM 3 (1896) 383-5. Krusch argued that this *Vita* was composed in the early ninth century; Beck (1950) XXXV, suggests that it was composed in the mid-sixth century.

[109] The chronology of Cyprian is uncertain; perhaps he lived in the mid-sixth century. His monastery was at Saint-Cyprien: see Vieillard-Troiekouroff (1976) 251.

some monks had a presentiment of this, they simultaneously threw
themselves before the tomb of the saint and began to pray. They said:
"O confessor saint, if you were still alive in this world you would be
able to rescue this poor man from the hand of death, just as you have
often freed those sentenced to such a punishment. But now we have no
doubts about your prayer, so that what you did while alive in this world
you are able to renew after being elevated to heaven." When night fell
the abbot sent [a monk] to the gallows. As the monk arrived, the
bindings immediately broke and the man fell to the ground. He was
supported by the monk and was brought, still alive, to the monastery.
After drinking a little wine he was better. Once the judge [i.e. the
count] pardoned his life, he left as a free man.[110]

100. Bishop Felix of Bourges.

After the death of bishop Felix of Bourges his tomb, which was
sculpted from Parian marble, was placed on top of the ground. When a
blind man, after his darkness vanished, received sight in his eyes at the
tomb of Felix, the people acknowledged him as a friend of God whom
they did not deserve to recognize fully when he was placed in a body
because the mists of this world were an obstacle. They began to cross
the threshold [of his shrine] because of the frequency of their prayers.
But since, as I said, the marble sarcophagus was covered with a less
expensive stone, the wisdom of the citizens and especially of the bishop
covered the sarcophagus with a better lid, that is, one made from Hera-
clean marble. When they removed the less expensive stone, they found
that the body of the confessor, almost twelve years after [his death], was
so untouched that no decay was found in the body and no corruption in
his clothing; but everything was so intact that, as I said, it was all
thought to have been placed in that tomb at that hour. But the
compassion of the Lord was not lacking there, so that the stone that

[110] When Gregory had eulogized the life and miracles of Eparchius upon his
death in 581, he also included another version of this story but with the
significant difference that Eparchius was still alive and negotiated directly with
the count [*HF* VI.8]. A *Vita* of Eparchius survives, composed probably in the
early ninth century: ed. B.Krusch, *MGH*, SRM 3 (1896) 553-60. On the basis
of details in this *Vita*, Krusch (1885) 811 n.3, argues that the version in *HF* was
more accurate that the version here in *GC*.

Tomb heals

was rejected did not remain without any glory. For some say that many people scratched off and drank a bit of dust from it, and as many were quickly delivered from quartan fevers as from tertian and daily fevers.[111]

101. Abbot Junianus of Limoges.

Junianus was a hermit in the territory of Limoges. While alive he revealed many miracles to the people; now ill people are often cured at his tomb. For I have seen many people, whom I think it too tedious to enumerate, who were brought there and received sight for their blind eyes or who were paralytics and were cured. These people offer proof. Today those who receive their health immediately make themselves subjects of this shrine, and after the cycle of another year rolls around they pay a contribution in gratitude for their health that was restored. Many of these people are seen to arrive at the church of my bishop, St Martin [of Tours].[112]

102. Pelagia of Limoges.

Pelagia was a devout ascetic and the mother of the blessed abbot Aredius whom I mentioned above. When she was oppressed by fevers and near death, she called her son and said: "I ask, my most beloved son, that you not bury me for four days, so that all the servants and maids might come and see my body and so that none of those whom I have most carefully supported might be excluded from my funeral." As she said this, she sent forth her spirit. After being washing according to custom she was placed on a bier and brought to the church. Before she was buried on the fourth day such a sweet fragrance flowed from her body that everyone was surprised. During the night a huge ball of fire appeared that rose in the east, moved across the circuit of the sky, and stopped over the church in which the body of the dead woman was

[111] Felix was bishop of Bourges during the later 560s and early 570s [*GM* 33], having succeeded Probianus [*GC* 79]: see Duchesne (1894-1915) II:28. Sulpicius, who served as bishop of Bourges from 584 [*HF* VI.39] until 591 [*HF* X.26], assisted in the enhancement of Felix's tomb, located in a church outside Bourges: see Vieillard-Troiekouroff (1976) 61-2.

[112] Junianus seems to have lived during the late fifth and early sixth centuries: see Vieillard-Troiekouroff (1976) 260, and Heinzelmann (1982) 632. A *Vita* of Junianus survives, composed probably during the ninth century or later: ed. B.Krusch, *MGH*, SRM 3 (1896) 377-9.

lying. The sudden brightness of this ball of fire so filled the entire church that people thought they saw the middle of the day. Immediately many possessed people cried out and said: "Martin [of Tours] has come to the funeral of Pelagia!" On the next Sunday after she was buried people placed a candle at her head and said: "Our candle is insufficient, for already the night is longer; when we rise for matins, then let this candle be burning." They closed the door and left. When their sleep was over, they entered the church and found that the candle that they had left extinguished was [now] burning. Often cures are performed for ill people at the tomb of this ascetic woman.[113]

103. The tomb of Criscentia at Paris.

In a village [in the territory] of Paris there was a tomb not far from the spot where, as some say, the church is called the "Senior Church". The tomb was not covered by a shelter. On the stone [tomb] was this inscription: "Here lies Criscentia, a girl dedicated to God." But no generation could remember of what value her merit had been and what she had done in this world. Recently, however, a cleric read this epitaph. Under the motivation of their faith men suspected that the virgin could have influence with the divine majesty. While they continued in this suspicion, a man whom the burning of a tertian fever was distressing with severe tremors scratched a bit of dust from the tomb and drank it; soon his tremors were calmed and he was well. The news was published and was of great benefit to many people afflicted with this illness. At a later time a man employed by the mint began to be seriously ill. A girl appeared to him in a vision and said: "Go as quickly as you can and cover the tomb of the virgin Criscentia. This deed will assist you so that you will not suffer long from the illness that holds you." The man believed, looked for limestone, and built an oratory over the tomb; immediately he was freed from his illness. But so that the power of the virgin might be exalted by greater honors, one man from the city had such a painful tooth that his jaw swelled and he was barely able to chew a small piece of tender food. Filled with faith he went to the tomb. He made a toothpick that was pointed on one end, as

[113] Pelagia died probably in 586, when "a shining light in the shape of a serpent" passed across the sky [*HF* VIII.42]. Her son Aredius was a friend of Gregory [*GC* 9].

it is usually made for cleaning teeth when used by people, and put it on
the tomb of the girl. As soon as it then touched the tooth that ached,
all the pain went numb. After the reception of this proof those whom
this pain bothered were soon cured when they sought the assistance of
her power.[114]

Toothache

104. The blessed Radegund of Poitiers.

The blessed Radegund, whom I mentioned at the beginning of my
book about martyrs, migrated from this world after completing the
labors of her life. After receiving the news of her death I went to the
convent at Poitiers that she had founded.[115] I found her lying on a bier;
her holy face was so bright that it surpassed the beauty of lilies and
roses. Standing around the bier was a large crowd of nuns, about two
hundred of them, who had converted because of Radegund's preaching
and adopted the holy life. According to the status of this world not
only were they [descended] from senators, but some were [descended]
from the royal family;[116] now they blossomed according to the rule of

---

[114] The identification of this church is uncertain. Perhaps Gregory here
referred to a church over the tomb of Marcellus [*GC* 87]: see Vieillard-
Troiekouroff (1976) 210, 215. Duval (1960) 108-9, prefers to read the girl's
name as Crescentia and dates the epitaph to the late fourth or early fifth century.

[115] Gregory elsewhere mentioned Radegund only occasionally. She was the
daughter of the king of Thuringia and was captured by king Chlothar in c.531,
who then married her. But after her husband had her brother killed, she left him,
became a nun, and founded a convent in Poitiers [*HF* III.7, IX.39-42]. There
Gregory sometimes visited her [*GM* 5]. Radegund died in 587 [cf. *HF* IX.2].

Two *Vitae* of Radegund survive. One was written by Fortunatus, her friend
who later became bishop of Poitiers: ed. B.Krusch, *MGH*, AA 4.2 (1885) 38-49,
and again in *MGH*, SRM 2 (1888) 364-77. The other was written by
Baudonivia, a nun who had lived in the convent during Radegund's lifetime: ed.
B.Krusch, *MGH*, SRM 2 (1888) 377-95.

[116] For her convent Radegund had adopted a monastic Rule composed by
Caesarius, bishop of Arles in the first half of the sixth century: see McCarthy
(1960), and Hochstetler (1987). She had also designated Agnes as abbess and
subordinated herself to her authority [*HF* IX.42]. But after the deaths of both, in
589 more than forty nuns revolted against the abbess Leubovera. Their leaders
were Chrodechildis and Basina, daughters of kings Charibert and Chilperic
respectively. When local bishops such as Gregory did not support their revolt,
Chrodechildis threatened to appeal to her royal relatives. Kings Guntramn and
Childebert II instead supported the bishops who excommunicated these

their piety. They stood there weeping and saying: "Holy mother, to whom will you leave us orphans? To whom do you entrust us who have been abandoned? We have left our parents, our possessions, and our homeland, and we have followed you. What will you leave us except perpetual tears and endless grief? Behold, until now this convent was more important for us than were the open spaces of villas or of cities. Wherever we went, when we saw your glorious face we found there gold and silver; there we saw blossoming vineyards, waving corn-fields, and meadows blooming with a variety of different flowers. From you we picked violets; for us, you were a glowing red rose and a brilliant lily. Your words shone for us like the sun; like the moon they illuminated a clear lamp of truth for the darkness of our conscience. Now, however, our entire world has been darkened and the area of this place has been constricted, since we do not deserve to see your face. Alas for us, who have been abandoned by our holy mother! Happy were those who migrated from this world while you were alive! We know that you have been admitted to the chorus of holy virgins and to the Paradise of God. Although we are consoled by that, the fact that we cannot see you with the eyes of our bodies is a reason for us to weep." They said these words and others while they wept.

When I was unable to restrain them from weeping, I turned to the abbess [Agnes] and said: "Cease for a little while from this weeping and instead prepare whatever is necessary. Behold, our brother Maroveus, the bishop of Poitiers, is not present because the task of visiting his parishes has detained him.[117] Now, however, form a plan

---

rebellious nuns [*HF* IX.39-43]. In 590 Chrodechildis resorted to violence and hired men to invade the convent, but again with royal support bishops excommunicated her and the other nuns [*HF* X.15-17]: see Scheibelreiter (1979), and Wallace-Hadrill (1983) 44-5, 55-7.

[117] Maroveus was bishop of Poitiers and a contemporary of Gregory: see Duchesne (1894-1915) II:83. He and Radegund kept their distance from each other; while Radegund was concerned lest he interfere in her convent [*HF* IX.42], he was probably only too aware of her royal patronage: see James (1982) 107-9. In 568-569 Radegund had acquired relics of the True Cross and of various saints from the imperial court in Constantinople [cf. *GM* 5]. When Maroveus would not preside at the transfer of these relics to her convent, bishop Eufronius of Tours substituted. Thereafter Maroveus refused to offer his protection to this convent in his diocese and did not attend Radegund's funeral. Although after her death he received a royal diploma granting him jurisdiction over the convent,

so that the holy body is not injured and so that the grace that God has bestowed on these holy limbs is not removed while the time of burial is delayed. Speed up the funeral that is due her, so that she might be placed in the tomb with honor." The abbess replied to these words: "But what will we do if the bishop of the city has not come? For the place where she ought to be buried has not been sanctified with the blessing of a bishop." Then the citizens and the other respected men who had come for the funeral of the blessed queen asked of my littleness and said: "Presume upon the love of your brother and bless this altar. For we trust in his goodwill that what you do will not offend him, but that he will be most grateful. Take [this task] upon yourself, we ask, so that the holy flesh might be placed in the tomb." So, since I was requested by them, I blessed the altar in her cell. But when we began to move the holy body and to escort it with the chanting of psalms, then possessed people shouted, acknowledged this saint of God, and said that she was tormenting them. As we passed by beneath the wall, a crowd of virgins began to cry and weep from the windows of the towers and from the tops of the fortifications of the wall, with the result that in the midst of the sobbing and the rejoicing of the psalms no one could keep themselves from weeping. The clerics too, whose duty was the chanting of psalms, could scarcely recite the antiphon because of their sobbing and weeping. Then we came to the tomb.[118] The foresight of the abbess had prepared a wooden casket in which she placed Radegund's body, packed in spices. The container for this entombment was therefore larger [than usual]; the casket was formed by removing one side from each of two tombs and then joining them together. Then the casket with the holy limbs was put in place. After offering a prayer I left, reserving for the local bishop [Maroveus the honor of] celebrating mass and covering the tomb with a lid.

I returned to the convent, and the abbess and the virgins led me to the particular spots where St Radegund had been accustomed to read or to pray. The abbess was weeping and said: "Behold, we are entering

se e note 117

---

lingering resentment against him also precipitated the revolt of the nuns [*HF* IX.40, 43].

[118] In the letter Radegund wrote to local bishops when she had founded her convent, she asked to be buried in the church of St Mary that she had constructed [*HF* IX.42]: see Vieillard-Troiekouroff (1976) 229-30.

her cell, but we do not find the mother who is lost! Behold the mat on which she bent her knees, wept, and prayed for the mercy of omnipotent God, but we do not see her! Behold the book in which she read, but her voice that was seasoned with a spiritual sharpness does not strike our ears! Behold the spindles on which she used to weave during her long fasts and while weeping copiously, but the beloved fingers of her holiness are not to be seen!" As they said this, they wept again and sighed, and even the internal organs of those weeping were dissolved in tears because of the emotion. Such grief overwhelmed my breast that I would not have stopped weeping if I did not realize that the blessed Radegund had departed from her convent in body but not in power, and that she had been taken from the world and placed in heaven.

105. Bishop Tetricus.

106. St Orientius, bishop.

107. The virgin Quiteria.[119]

108. St Paulinus, bishop.

Paulinus was a man with a [distinguished] life. He was descended from a noble family [and became bishop of] Nola. He chose Therasia as a wife who was comparable to himself. He possessed much wealth and was as wealthy in the ownership of estates as he was reliable in the protection of his homes. There is a passage from the Gospels in which

[119] Although Gregory included these three headings in his table of contents for the *GC*, no extant manuscripts contain the chapters; Krusch (1885) 816 n.1, suggests that perhaps Gregory's death prevented him from composing the actual chapters. Tetricus was a great-uncle of Gregory. He had succeeded his father, bishop Gregorius of Langres [*GM* 50, *VP* 7], in c.540 and served as bishop until c.573; Gregory may have written another "small book" about him [*HF* IV.16]. Orientius was bishop of Auch in the early and mid-fifth century and a poet: see Griffe (1964-1966) I:19-20, 31-4, 276-7. A *Vita* of Orientius survives, composed perhaps in the early sixth century: ed. *Acta Sanctorum*, Maius I (1866) 62-3. Quiteria is unknown. According to a later account, after being decapitated as a martyr in Spain at the end of the fifth century she had carried her head some miles before being buried. A marble sarcophagus attributed to Quiteria has been found at Aire-sur-l'Adour: see Vieillard-Troiekouroff (1976) 27-8.

the Lord criticized a young man for his wealth and said: "Go, sell all that you have and give to the poor, and you will have treasure in heaven; and come, follow me. It is easier for a camel to pass through the eye of a needle than for a rich man to enter the kingdom of God" [Matthew 19:21, 24]. As soon as this passage entered Paulinus' ears, he immediately sold all that he had and donated it to the poor. Relieved of all his desires, he freely followed his master. In this way he thought that he might be enriched by the wealth of Paradise, if he was seen to possess nothing transitory. Divine majesty assisted him, so that what [the Lord] had said in the Gospel was impossible, Paulinus deserved to make possible and perform in his actions. Once a man who requested a donation came to him, and Paulinus said to his wife: "Go and give him what he considers necessary." His wife replied: "We have no more than one loaf of bread." Paulinus said to her: "Go and give it away. The Lord will give us food." But Therasia, like a conscientious woman, wanted the bread to be kept, lest she have nothing, and did not want to give it away. Then some men came and said that they had been sent by their masters to bring Paulinus a gift of grain and wine. They said they had been delayed because a storm that arose had carried off one of their ships with its wheat. The man of God turned to his wife and said: "Be aware that because you stole one loaf from that poor man, this ship was sunk."

As if about to make a pilgrimage he set out with his wife for another region; he possessed nothing except his own rank. Much later when the inhabitants of his own region looked for him, he could not be found at all. A merchant from that city went to the city where the blessed man was serving the celestial Lord. When he saw Paulinus, immediately he threw himself to the ground, embraced the feet of the saint, and said: "This is the blessed Paulinus, who is known to the entire world but who could not be found at all when sought at length by his own citizens." The merchant told of all of Paulinus' actions, and those who listened were amazed. When the bishop of Nola died, immediately Paulinus was selected as his successor. Because this church possessed much wealth, the Lord fulfilled in Paulinus what he had deigned to promise in the Gospel: "He who will have abandoned everything for my sake will receive a hundred-fold in this world and will possess eternal life in the future" [Matthew 19:29]. But once he assumed the episcopacy, Paulinus always presented himself as a humble man, because he knew that he would be exalted in the presence of God if he pursued humility. The income from the church's revenues that his hand touched was immediately donated to the poor. His most chaste wife never disagreed with him.[120]

Paulinus was a holy man [noted] for his marvelous discretion and educated in rhetorical skills. His literary corpus, so far as it is extant for me, truly demonstrates his skill. He wrote on various subjects in verse as well as in prose. He wrote six books in verse about the miracles of the blessed Martin and some other short poems in praise of Martin. For Paulinus saw Martin when he was alive in his body, and he received sight in his own eye from Martin. Because Paulinus had increased the gifts of his spiritual favors, he was so distinguished for his power that at his death, before he gave up his spirit, he saw with the eyes of his body Martin and Genuarius of Italy, who had migrated from this world before Paulinus.[121]

Because I have read nothing about the life of the blessed Paulinus, I am relating what I learned from an account of trustworthy men when I

[120] Paulinus was a member of a noted Gallic family and had served briefly in the imperial administration before committing himself to a more ascetic form of Christianity at the end of the fourth century. Eventually he moved to Nola, a small town near Naples in Italy, where he subsequently served as bishop until his death in 431: see Frend (1969), Brown (1981) 53-68, and Van Dam (1985) 303-11. Gregory seems to have been attracted enough to the example of Paulinus that he concluded this book with a chapter about Paulinus and his book about the martyrs with a chapter about St Felix, the patron saint of Nola whose cult Paulinus had promoted [GM 103].

[121] Sulpicius Severus, Vita Martini 19.3, ed. C.Halm, CSEL 1 (1866) 128, and trans. A.Roberts, NPNF 2nd series, 11 (reprinted 1973) 13, had already recorded how bishop Martin of Tours had once healed Paulinus; Uranius, Epistola de obitu S. Paulini ad Pacatum (PL 53.859-66), to whose account of Paulinus' death Gregory here referred, mentioned that on his deathbed Paulinus had conversed with St Martin and St Genuarius (or Januarius), a bishop and martyr of Naples. Paulinus wrote many letters and poems, and Gregory excerpted some of the latter composed in honor of St Felix [GM 103]: ed. G.de Hartel, CSEL 29-30 (1894), and trans. P.G.Walsh, ACW 35-36, 40 (1966-1975). But Gregory was mistaken, here and elsewhere [VM 1.2], in attributing to Paulinus of Nola the authorship of a long poem, in six books, that had versified first the writings of Sulpicius Severus about St Martin and then an account of miracles that St Martin had performed after his death. In fact, Paulinus of Périgueux had composed this poem in the mid-fifth century: ed. M.Petschenig, CSEL 16.1 (1888) 17-159, with Van Dam (1986).

wished to speak of his almsgiving. Because I have a long account of Paulinus' death, I have therefore not repeated it in turn. Behold what almsgiving offers! Behold what treasures God bestows upon his saints who give themselves to the poor! In contrast, he removes from those who lust in the evil of avarice that which they wickedly covet, in accordance with the saying in the sacred Gospel: "To him who has it will be given, and he will have abundance; but from him who has not, what he seems to have will be taken away" [Matthew 13:12, 25:29].

109. The merchant who did not give alms.

The account of many people confirms that this happened somewhere in a port on the sea. A poor man who was old and weighed down with bags came to the seacoast. He went to the port and began to seek alms from ship-owners. He repeatedly begged from a man who was captain of a ship and said: "Give me something." The other man was upset and said: "Stop it, I ask of you, decrepit old man, and do not beg me for anything; for here [in this ship] we have nothing expect stones." The poor man replied: "If you say that the ship in your command contains stones, then everything will be changed into stones." And immediately the entire cargo of the ship, whatever could be eaten, was changed to stone. I myself saw dates from this cargo, and I saw olives that were harder than marble. For although they were changed into the hardness of a stone, they never lost the color they had had, and both shape and appearance remained the same. Although the captain of the ship was moved to repentance, he could never find the old man whom he sought. Some say that he sent [a sample] from the goods that were changed to stone for viewing in many cities, so that it might be an example for everyone that they not do the same. Behold what you do, shameless greediness! You have made a pauper out of a man who thought he could become wealthier by not giving something to a poor man.

110. Another [merchant] who diluted his wine.

I will not pass over what happened to another man who wished to increase his worldly profits by counterfeiting. At Lyon a man who worked [only] reluctantly so that he could acquire one small gold coin

burned with an impious lust for accursed gold and wished to fill the
mouth of a sack with gold, in accordance with that line by our [poet]
Prudentius: "As gold is amassed, the lust for gold is enhanced."[122] So
he purchased wine with this small gold coin, mixed it with water, sold
it for silver coins, and doubled his money. He did this again and again,
and he pursued evil profit long enough until he accumulated one hundred large gold coins from this one small gold coin. But the judgement
of God restrained the profits of the devil. Although he was to possess
his money for the short time of one hour, the greedy merchant collected
his gold in a sack and went to the market of another merchant. He took
out a small gold coin as if he were about to purchase something and
began to talk with his friend. His sack was made from Phoenician [i.e.
purple-red] leather, like those it is customary to carry in one's hand.
And behold, suddenly a hawk came, seized the sack with his claws, and,
thinking from the color that it was a piece of flesh, tried to tear it. But
when the bird realized there was no meat in the sack, it flew over the
Saône river—from which the man had drained water to mix with his
wine—, released the sack, and dropped it in the river. The man pulled
his hair, threw himself to the ground, sprinkled dust over his head, and
said: "Woe am I, who am crushed by the judgement of God and have
lost the money that was collected unjustly! For I accumulated one
hundred large gold coins from one small gold coin. Now that the one
hundred large coins are lost, only this one small gold coin remains for
me. Woe am I; as I have done, so I have received. I who acquired these
coins from nothing see them returned to nothing!"

Devil, such money is yours, and through such profits you lead
those who obey you to hell. Such a transaction inflicts the mark of
condemnation in the present and produces varieties of different punish-
ments in the future. I ask that you who read these words cease from
these activities, cease and do not participate in such behavior! Let the
favor of divine majesty be your profit; let the teaching of the sacred
Scripture be your occupation! Let your association be with the purses
of the poor that extinguish the raging fire of eternal hell! This goal
must not be sought by one's own power, but must be requested from
the pity of the Lord, who deigns to answer us because of the holy

---

[122] Quoted inaccurately from Prudentius, *Hamartigenia* 257, ed. and trans.
H.J.Thomson, LCL (1949-1953) I: 222-3.

intercession of those [saints] whose holy miracles this book reveals. Then, by making a good account not only regarding our earthly wealth but also regarding the talents [mentioned] in his parable, after receiving the reward for multiplying [our wealth] may we deserve to hear the Lord say: "Well done, faithful servant. Because you have been faithful over a little, I will set you over much; enter into the joy of your Lord" [Matthew 25:21].

BIBLIOGRAPHY

Anson, J. (1974). "The female transvestite in early monasticism: the origin and development of a motif," *Viator* 5, pp.1-32.

Banniard, M. (1978). "L'aménagement de l'histoire chez Grégoire de Tours: à propos de l'invasion de 451 (*H.L.*II 5-7)," *Romano-barbarica* 3, pp.5-37.

Barnes, T.D. (1981). *Constantine and Eusebius* (Cambridge, Massachusetts).

Baus, K., H.-G.Beck, E.Ewig, and H.J.Vogt (1980). *The imperial Church from Constantine to the early Middle Ages. = History of the Church*, ed. H.Jedin and J.Dolan, vol.2, trans. A.Biggs (New York).

Beck, H.G.J. (1950). *The pastoral care of souls in south-east France during the sixth century* (Rome).

Biraben, J.-N. and J.Le Goff (1975). "The plague in the early Middle Ages," in *Biology of man in history*, ed. R.Forster and O.Ranum, trans. E.Forster and P.M.Ranum (Baltimore) 48-80.

Bonnet, M. (1890). *Le Latin de Grégoire de Tours* (Paris).

Brennan, B. (1985). "The career of Venantius Fortunatus," *Traditio* 41, pp.49-78.

———. (1985a). "'Episcopae': bishops' wives viewed in sixth-century Gaul," *Church History* 54, pp.311-23.

Brown, P. (1981). *The cult of the saints. Its rise and function in Latin Christianity* (Chicago).

Buchner, R. (1955). "Einleitung," in *Gregor von Tours, Zehn Bücher Geschichten*, ed. and trans. R.Buchner (Darmstadt, 4th ed.) I: VII-LI.

Bynum, C.W. (1987). *Holy feast and holy fast. The religious significance of food to medieval women* (Berkeley).

Chadwick, O. (1948). "Gregory of Tours and Gregory the Great," *Journal of Theological Studies* 49, pp.38-49.

Clark, E.A. (1982). "Claims on the bones of Saint Stephen: the partisans of Melania and Eudocia," *Church History* 51, pp.141-56. Reprinted in her *Ascetic piety and women's faith. Essays on late ancient Christianity.* Studies in Women and Religion 20 (Lewiston, 1986) 95-123.

Collins, R. (1980). "Mérida and Toledo: 550-585," in *Visigothic Spain: new approaches,* ed. E.James (Oxford) 189-219.

_____. (1983). *Early medieval Spain: unity in diversity, 400-1000* (London).

Courcelle, P. (1964). *Histoire littéraire des grandes invasions germaniques* (Paris, 3rd ed.).

Dalton, O.M. (1927). *The history of the Franks by Gregory of Tours* (Oxford), 2 vols. [I: Introduction; II: Translation and notes].

Delehaye, H. (1927). *Sanctus. Essai sur le culte des saints dans l'antiquité.* Subsidia hagiographica 17 (Brussels).

Dolbeau, F. (1983). "La vie en prose de saint Marcel, évêque de Die. Histoire du texte et édition critique," *Francia* 11, pp.97-130.

Duchesne, L. (1894-1915). *Fastes épiscopaux de l'ancienne Gaule* (Paris), 3 vols.

Duval, P.-M. (1960), ed. *Les inscriptions antiques de Paris,* vol.1 (Paris).

Elbern, V.H. (1966). "HIC SCS SYMION. Eine vorkarolingische Kultstatue des Symeon Stylites in Poitiers," *Cahiers archéologiques* 16, pp.23-38.

Ewig, E. (1961). "Le culte de Saint Martin à l'époque franque," *Revue d'histoire de l'église de France* 47, pp.1-18. Reprinted in his *Spätantikes und fränkisches Gallien. Gesammelte Schriften (1952-1973),* ed. H.Atsma, vol.2 (Munich, 1979) 355-70.

_____. (1974). "Studien zur merowingischen Dynastie," *Frühmittelalterliche Studien* 8, pp.15-59.

_____. (1978). "Bemerkungen zur Vita des Bischofs Lupus von Troyes," in *Geschichtsschreibung und geistiges Leben im Mittelalter. Festschrift für Heinz Löwe zum 65. Geburtstag,* ed. K.Hauck and J.Mordek (Cologne) 14-26.

Fontaine, J. (1967-1969), ed. and trans. *Sulpice Sévère, Vie de saint Martin.* SChr.133-135 (Paris), 3 vols.

_____. (1976). "Hagiographie et politique, de Sulpice Sévère à Venance Fortunat," *Revue d'histoire de l'église de France* 62, pp.113-40.

Fournier, P.-F. (1955). "La persistance du Gaulois au VIᵉ siècle d'après Grégoire de Tours," in *Recueil de travaux offert à M. Clovis Brunel* (Paris) I:448-53.

_____. (1979). "Saint Austremoine premier évêque de Clermont. Son épiscopat, ses reliques, ses legendes," *Bulletin historique et scientifique de l'Auvergne* 89, pp.417-71.

Frend, W.H.C. (1969). "Paulinus of Nola and the last century of the western empire," *Journal of Roman Studies* 59, pp.1-11. Reprinted in his *Town and country in the early Christian centuries* (London, 1980), Chap.XIV.

Gauthier, N. (1980). *L'évangélisation des pays de la Moselle. La province romaine de Première Belgique entre antiquité et Moyen-Age (IIIᵉ—VIIIᵉ siècles)* (Paris).

Geary, P.J. (1988). *Before France and Germany. The creation and transformation of the Merovingian world* (Oxford).

Gilliard, F.D. (1975). "The apostolicity of Gallic churches," *Harvard Theological Review* 68, pp.17-33.

Goffart, W. (1987). "From *Historiae* to *Historia Francorum* and back again: aspects of the textual history of Gregory of Tours," in *Religion, culture, and society in the early Middle Ages. Studies in honor of Richard E. Sullivan*, ed. T.F.X.Noble and J.J.Contreni (Kalamazoo) 55-76.

Gras, P. (1955). "Le séjour à Dijon des évêques de Langres du Vᵉ au IXᵉ siècle. Ses consequences sur l'histoire de la ville," in *Recueil de travaux offert à M. Clovis Brunel* (Paris) I:550-61.

des Graviers, J. (1946). "La date du commencement de l'année chez Grégoire de Tours," *Revue d'histoire de l'église de France* 32, pp.103-6.

Griffe, E. (1955). "Les origines chrétiennes de la Gaule et les légendes clémentines," *Bulletin de littérature ecclésiastique* 56, pp.3-22.

_____. (1964-1966). *La Gaule chrétienne à l'époque romaine* (Paris, rev.ed.), 3 vols.

Heinzelmann, M. (1981). "Une source de base de la littérature hagiographique latine: le recueil de miracles," in *Hagiographie, cultures et sociétés IVᵉ—XIIᵉ siècles. Actes du Colloque organisé à Nanterre et à Paris (2-5 mai 1979)* (Paris) 235-57.

    _____. (1982). "Gallische Prosopographie 260-527," *Francia* 10, pp.531-718.

    _____, and J.-C.Poulin (1986). *Les vies anciennes de sainte Geneviève de Paris. Etudes critiques.* Bibliothèque de l'Ecole des Hautes Etudes, IVᵉ section, sciences historiques et philologiques 329 (Paris).

Hochstetler, D. (1987). "The meaning of monastic cloister for women according to Caesarius of Arles," in *Religion, culture, and society in the early Middle Ages. Studies in honor of Richard E. Sullivan,* ed. T.F.X.Noble and J.J.Contreni (Kalamazoo) 27-40.

Hunt, E.D. (1982). *Holy Land pilgrimage in the later Roman empire AD 312-460* (Oxford).

James, E. (1982). *The origins of France. From Clovis to the Capetians, 500-1000* (New York).

    _____. (1983). "'Beati pacifici': bishops and the law in sixth-century Gaul," in *Disputes and settlements. Law and human relations in the West,* ed. J.Bossy (Cambridge) 25-46.

    _____. (1985), trans. *Gregory of Tours, Life of the Fathers* (Liverpool).

Krusch, B. (1885). "Georgii Florentii Gregorii episcopi Turonensis libri octo miraculorum," in *MGH*, SRM 1 (Hannover) 451-820 [Introduction, edition of text, and notes].

    _____. (1951). "Gregorii episcopi Turonensis decem libri historiarum. Praefatio," in *MGH*, SRM 1.1, editio altera, fasc.3 (Hannover) IX-XXII.

Kurth, G. (1919). *Etudes franques* (Paris and Brussels), 2 vols.

Le Goff, J. (1980). "Clerical culture and folklore traditions in Merovingian civilization," in his *Time, work, and culture in the Middle Ages,* trans. A.Goldhammer (Chicago) 153-8.

    _____. (1980a). "Ecclesiastical culture and folklore in the Middle Ages: Saint Marcellus of Paris and the dragon," in his *Time, work, and culture in the Middle Ages*, trans. A.Goldhammer (Chicago) 159-88.

Lelong, C. (1960). "De l'importance du pélerinage de Tours au VIe siècle," *Bulletin trimestriel de la Société archéologique de Touraine* 32, pp.232-7.

Levillain, L. (1927). "Saint Trophime, confesseur et métropolitain de Arles, et la mission des Sept en Gaule," *Revue d'histoire de l'église de France* 13, pp.145-89.

Lot, F. (1929). "La *Vita Viviani* et la domination visigothique en Aquitaine," in *Mélanges Paul Fournier* (Paris) 467-77. Reprinted in his *Recueil des travaux historiques de Ferdinand Lot*, vol.2 (Geneva, 1970) 101-11.

Mandouze, A. (1982). *Prosopographie de l'Afrique chrétienne (303-533).* = *Prosopographie chrétienne du Bas-Empire*, vol.1 (Paris).

Mathisen, R.W. (1982). "PLRE II: suggested *addenda* and *corrigenda*," *Historia* 31, pp.364-86.

_____. (1987). "Some hagiographical addenda to *P.L.R.E.*," *Historia* 36, pp.448-461.

McCarthy, M.C. (1960). *The Rule for nuns of St. Caesarius of Arles. A translation with a critical introduction* (Washington, D.C.).

McDermott, W.C. (1975). "Bishops: the world of Gregory of Tours," in *Monks, bishops and pagans. Christian culture in Gaul and Italy, 500-700*, ed. E.Peters (Philadelphia) 117-218.

_____. (1975a). "Felix of Nantes: a Merovingian bishop," *Traditio* 31, pp.1-24.

Meyer, W. (1901). *Der Gelegenheitsdichter Venantius Fortunatus.* Abhandlungen der königlichen Gesellschaft der Wissenschaften zu Göttingen, philologisch-historische Klasse, neue Folge, Band IV no.5 (Berlin).

Mitchell, K. (1987). "Saints and public Christianity in the *Historiae* of Gregory of Tours," in *Religion, culture, and society in the early Middle Ages. Studies in honor of Richard E. Sullivan*, ed. T.F.X.Noble and J.J.Contreni (Kalamazoo) 77-94.

Monod, G. (1872). *Etudes critiques sur les sources de l'histoire mérovingienne*, vol.1 (Paris).

de Nie, G. (1985). "The spring, the seed and the tree: Gregory of Tours on the wonders of nature," *Journal of Medieval History* 11, pp.89-135. Reprinted in her *Views from a many-windowed tower. Studies of imagination in the works of Gregory of Tours* (Amsterdam, 1987) 71-132.

Patlagean, E. (1976). "L'histoire de la femme déguisée en moine et l'évolution de la sainteté féminine à Byzance," *Studi medievali*, ser.3, 17, pp.597-623. Reprinted in her *Structure sociale, famille, chrétienté à Byzance, IVe—XIe siècle* (London, 1981) Chap.XI.

Pietri, L. (1983). *La ville de Tours du IVe au VIe siècle: naissance d'une cité chrétienne* (Rome).

_____. (1983a). "Les abbés de basilique dans la Gaule du VIe siècle," *Revue d'histoire de l'église de France* 69, pp.5-28.

Prieur, J.-M. (1981). "La figure de l'apôtre dans les Actes apocryphes d'André," in *Les Actes apocryphes des apôtres. Christianisme et monde païen*, ed. F.Bovon et al. (Geneva) 121-39.

Riché, P. (1976). *Education and culture in the barbarian West sixth through eighth centuries*, trans. J.J.Contreni (Columbia).

Rouche, M. (1979). *L'Aquitaine des Wisigoths aux Arabes. Naissance d'une région* (Paris).

Scheibelreiter, G. (1979). "Königstöchter im Kloster. Radegund (†587) und der Nonnenaufstand von Poitiers (589)," *Mitteilungen des Instituts für österreichische Geschichtsforschung* 87, pp.1-37.

Schlick, J. (1966). "Composition et chronologie des *De virtutibus sancti Martini* de Grégoire de Tours," *Studia Patristica* 7 = *Texte und Untersuchungen* 92, pp.278-86.

Selle-Hosbach, K. (1974). *Prosopographie merowingischer Amtsträger in der Zeit von 511 bis 613* (Bonn).

Stancliffe, C. (1983). *St. Martin and his hagiographer. History and miracle in Sulpicius Severus* (Oxford).

Stock, B. (1983). *The implications of literacy. Written language and models of interpretation in the eleventh and twelfth centuries* (Princeton).

van der Straeten, J. (1974). "Vie inédite de S. Memmie premier évêque de Chalons-sur-Marne," *Analecta Bollandiana* 92, pp.297-319.

Stroheker, K.F. (1948). *Der senatorische Adel im spätantiken Gallien* (Tubingen).

Thompson, E.A. (1969). *The Goths in Spain* (Oxford).

_____. (1984). *Saint Germanus of Auxerre and the end of Roman Britain* (Woodbridge).

Thorpe, L. (1974), trans. *Gregory of Tours, The history of the Franks* (Harmondsworth).

Van Dam, R. (1985). *Leadership and community in late antique Gaul* (Berkeley).

_____. (1986). "Paulinus of Périgueux and Perpetuus of Tours," *Francia* 14, pp.567-73.

_____. (1988), trans. *Gregory of Tours, Glory of the martyrs* (Liverpool).

_____. (1988a). "Images of St.Martin in late Roman and early Merovingian Gaul," *Viator* 19, pp.1-27.

Vieillard-Troiekouroff, M. (1976). *Les monuments religieux de la Gaule d'après les oeuvres de Grégoire de Tours* (Paris).

Vollmann, B.K. (1983). "Gregory IV (Gregory von Tours)," in *Reallexikon für Antike und Christentum*, ed. T.Klauser et al., vol.12 (Stuttgart), col.895-930.

Wallace-Hadrill, J.M. (1967). *The barbarian West 400-1000* (London, 3rd ed.).

_____. (1983). *The Frankish Church* (Oxford).

Weidemann, M. (1982). *Kulturgeschichte der Merowingerzeit nach den Werken Gregors von Tours* (Mainz), 2 vols.

Wood, I.N. (1979). "Early Merovingian devotion in town and country," in *The Church in town and countryside*, ed. D.Baker. *Studies in Church History* 16 (Oxford) 61-76.

_____. (1981). "A prelude to Columbanus: the monastic achievement in the Burgundian territories," in *Columbanus and Merovingian monasticism*, ed. H.B.Clarke and M.Brennan. BAR International Series 113 (Oxford) 3-32.

_____. (1983). "The ecclesiastical politics of Merovingian Clermont," in *Ideal and reality in Frankish and Anglo-Saxon society. Studies presented to J.M.Wallace-Hadrill*, ed. P.Wormald, D.Bullough, and R.Collins (Oxford) 34-57.

_____. (1984). "The end of Roman Britain: continental evidence and parallels," in *Gildas: new approaches*, ed. M.Lapidge and D.Dumville. *Studies in Celtic History* 5 (Woodbridge) 1-25.

_____. (1985). "Gregory of Tours and Clovis," *Revue belge de philologie et d'histoire* 63, pp.249-72.

_____. (1986). "Disputes in late fifth- and sixth-century Gaul: some problems," in *The settlement of disputes in early medieval Europe*, ed. W.Davies and P.Fouracre (Cambridge) 7-22.

Zelzer, K. (1977). "Zur Frage des Autors der Miracula B. Andreae Apostoli und zur Sprache des Gregor von Tours," *Grazer Beiträge* 6, pp.217-41.

INDEX

ASSOCIATION INTERNATIONALE D'ETUDES PATRISTIQUES

International Association

for Patristic Studies

The Association exists to promote Patristic Studies in various ways. Its chief activity is to compile and publish annually a list of present and future patristic actvity, both in the form of research projects and conferences. It also provides a list of members and their fields of interest.

The purpose of these published Bulletins is to enable scholarship to advance with maximum co-operation and without unnecessary repetition and overlap. It is also envisaged that the discipline itself may be promoted by consultation in various other ways.

For further details please write to:

Professor the Revd. S.G. Hall
Department of Christian Doctrine and History
King's College London (KQC)
Strand
London WC2R 2LS